n, Kansas City, Missouri | 7th & Locust, Des Moines, Iowa | 12th & Baltimore, Kansas City, Missouri | 12th and Walnut, Kansas City, Missouri | 40th & Mo
n, Missouri | 15th & Cleveland, Kansas City, Missouri | 3030 Prospect, Kansas City, Missouri | Independence & Hardesty, Kansas City, Linwood
Edmond, St. Joseph, Missouri | 8th & Washington, St. Louis, Missouri | Manchester & Sutton, Maplewood, Missouri | Kansas C
as | 954 Minnesota, Kansas City, Kansas | 50th & May, Oklahoma City, Oklahoma | 4701 Sycamore, Roeland Pc Des Moi
124 Raytown Road, Kansas City, Missouri | 100 E. Euclid, Des Moines, Iowa | 1925 S. Third, Memphis, Tennessee | 1 ew, Misso
2 Prospect, Kansas City, Missouri | 460 N. Lindberg, Florissant, Missouri | 1735 S. Glenstone, Springfield, Missouri | 1635 Poplar, Memphis, Tennessee | K
on & Elm, St. Louis, Missouri | 7401 Manchester, St. Louis, Missouri | 8th & Grand, Kansas City, Missouri | 12th and McGee, Kansas City, Missouri | 728 Mir
Missouri | 12th and Walnut, Kansas City, Missouri | 40th & Main, Kansas City, Missouri | 4th & Pierce, Sioux City, Iowa | Main & Robinson, Oklahoma Ci
ouri | Independence & Hardesty, Kansas City, Missouri | Linwood & Troost, Kansas City, Missouri | 63rd & Brookside, Kansas City, Missouri | 6150 Natur
tton, Maplewood, Missouri | Independence & Prospect, Kansas City, Missouri | Armour & Swift, North Kansas City, Missouri | Gregory & Prospect, Kansa
| 4701 Sycamore, Roeland Park, Kansas | 1900 Carpenter, Des Moines, Iowa | 2256 Lamar, Memphis, Tennessee | 441 N. Kirkwood, Kirkwood, Missouri
25 S. Third, Memphis, Tennessee | 12236 S. 71 Highway, Grandview, Missouri | 31st & Van Brunt, Kansas City, Missouri | 7501 Metcalf, Overland Park, Ka
Glenstone, Springfield, Missouri | 1635 Poplar, Memphis, Tennessee | Katz Drugs, Sedalia, Missouri | Katz Drugs, Hutchinson, Kansas | East Hills Regiona
nd, Kansas City, Missouri | 12th and McGee, Kansas City, Missouri | 728 Minnesota, Kansas City, Kansas | 601 Francis, St. Joseph, Missouri | 10th & Mai
Missouri | 4th & Pierce, Sioux City, Iowa | Main & Robinson, Oklahoma City, Oklahoma | 7th & Locust, St. Louis, Missouri | Hodiamont & Easton, Wellsto
as City, Missouri | 63rd & Brookside, Kansas City, Missouri | 6150 Natural Bridge, Pine Lawn, Missouri | 75th & Broadway, Kansas City, Missouri | 6th and
uri | Armour & Swift, North Kansas City, Missouri | Gregory & Prospect, Kansas City, Missouri | 201 N. Main, Independence, Missouri | 52nd & Roe, Missi
a | 2256 Lamar, Memphis, Tennessee | 441 N. Kirkwood, Kirkwood, Missouri | 9005 E. 50 Highway, Raytown, Missouri | 8959 Riverview Blvd., St. Louis, Miss
st & Van Brunt, Kansas City, Missouri | 7501 Metcalf, Overland Park, Kansas | 115 W. 29th, Topeka, Kansas | 8571 Watson Road, Webster Groves, Misso
s, Sedalia, Missouri | Katz Drugs, Hutchinson, Kansas | East Hills Regional Shopping Center, St. Joseph, Missouri | Elms Shopping Center, Joplin, Missouri
a, Kansas City, Kansas | 601 Francis, St. Joseph, Missouri | 10th & Main, Kansas City, Missouri | 7th & Locust, Des Moines, Iowa | 12th & Baltimore, Kans
ahoma | 7th & Locust, St. Louis, Missouri | Hodiamont & Easton, Wellston, Missouri | 15th & Cleveland, Kansas City, Missouri | 3030 Prospect, Kansas C
Pine Lawn, Missouri | 75th & Broadway, Kansas City, Missouri | 6th and Edmond, St. Joseph, Missouri | 8th & Washington, St. Louis, Missouri | Manchest
souri | 201 N. Main, Independence, Missouri | 52nd & Roe, Mission, Kansas | 954 Minnesota, Kansas City, Kansas | 50th & May, Oklahoma City, Oklaho
ighway, Raytown, Missouri | 8959 Riverview Blvd., St. Louis, Missouri | 3124 Raytown Road, Kansas City, Missouri | 100 E. Euclid, Des Moines, Iowa | 192
, Topeka, Kansas | 8571 Watson Road, Webster Groves, Missouri | 6312 Prospect, Kansas City, Missouri | 460 N. Lindberg, Florissant, Missouri | 1735 S. Gl
St. Joseph, Missouri | Elms Shopping Center, Joplin, Missouri | Watson & Elm, St. Louis, Missouri | 7401 Manchester, St. Louis, Missouri | 8th & Grand, Kans
7th & Locust, Des Moines, Iowa | 12th & Baltimore, Kansas City, Missouri | 12th and Walnut, Kansas City, Missouri | 40th & Main, Kansas City, Missouri |
nd, Kansas City, Missouri | 3030 Prospect, Kansas City, Missouri | Independence & Hardesty, Kansas City, Missouri | Linwood & Troost, Kansas City, Miss
ri | 8th & Washington, St. Louis, Missouri | Manchester & Sutton, Maplewood, Missouri | Independence & Prospect, Kansas City, Missouri | Armour & S
nsas City, Kansas | 50th & May, Oklahoma City, Oklahoma | 4701 Sycamore, Roeland Park, Kansas | 1900 Carpenter, Des Moines, Iowa | 2256 Lamo
Kansas City, Missouri | 100 E. Euclid, Des Moines, Iowa | 1925 S. Third, Memphis, Tennessee | 12236 S. 71 Highway, Grandview, Missouri | 31st & Van Bru
, City, Missouri | 460 N. Lindberg, Florissant, Missouri | 1735 S. Glenstone, Springfield, Missouri | 1635 Poplar, Memphis, Tennessee | Katz Drugs, Sedalia
is, Missouri | 7401 Manchester, St. Louis, Missouri | 8th & Grand, Kansas City, Missouri | 12th and McGee, Kansas City, Missouri | 728 Minnesota, Kansas
Walnut, Kansas City, Missouri | 40th & Main, Kansas City, Missouri | 4th & Pierce, Sioux City, Iowa | Main & Robinson, Oklahoma City, Oklahoma | 7t
e & Hardesty, Kansas City, Missouri | Linwood & Troost, Kansas City, Missouri | 63rd & Brookside, Kansas City, Missouri | 6150 Natural Bridge, Pine Lawn
Missouri | Independence & Prospect, Kansas City, Missouri | Armour & Swift, North Kansas City, Missouri | Gregory & Prospect, Kansas City, Missouri |
oeland Park, Kansas | 1900 Carpenter, Des Moines, Iowa | 2256 Lamar, Memphis, Tennessee | 441 N. Kirkwood, Kirkwood, Missouri | 9005 E. 50 Highw

65 stores

5 states

$100,000,000 in annual sales

$1.3 million annual sales volume per store

255,000 customers a day

3,000 employees, from soda jerks to vice presidents

120 registered pharmacists

268,000 tickets given free to Kansas City Philharmonic concerts

70,000 tickets given free to Kansas City Blues baseball games

75,000 square feet in biggest store

100 pages of newspaper ads,
16 billboards and 52 bus placards
for opening of Springfield, Missouri store

57 years

THE KINGS OF CUT-RATE

THE KINGS OF CUT-RATE

THE VERY AMERICAN STORY OF ISAAC AND MICHAEL KATZ

BY BRIAN BURNES WITH STEVE KATZ

★ KANSAS CITY STAR BOOKS

IKE AND MIKE KATZ WERE LIKE ALCHEMISTS.
BOTH HAD THE KNACK OF TURNING
OBSTACLES INTO OPPORTUNITIES.

Published by Kansas City Star Books
1729 Grand Boulevard
Kansas City, Missouri 64108
Kansascity.com
Copyright © 2011 The Kansas City Star Co.
and Steve Katz

First Edition, First Printing

ISBN: 978-1-935362-67-8
Library of Congress number: 2010931075

Editor and project manager:
Carol Powers

Book designer:
DJ Hyde Matheny, the ping pong studio

Chapter opening illustrations:
DJ Hyde Matheny

Tabletop photography and spot photography
of memorabilia: Aaron Leimkuehler, photographer,
The Kansas City Star; DJ Hyde Matheny, art director

Dust jacket photo: The first Katz Drug Store at
12th and McGee, courtesy of the Katz family.

i Mortar and Pestle: Photo by Aaron Leimkuehler,
The Kansas City Star

iv – v Background photo: Katz Drug store on
Independence Square, Independence, Missouri, 1950,
by L.D. Jones, courtesy of the Harry S. Truman
Library and Museum

viii - ix Background photo: Interior of the Katz Drug
store at Linwood and Troost, Kansas City, Missouri,
1941, courtesy of the Missouri Valley Special
Collections, Kansas City Public Library, Kansas City,
Missouri

All the photographs in this book, except those
individually credited, came from The Kansas City Star
and the Katz family archives. With few exceptions,
the historic records, objects and memorabilia came
from Katz family collections.

**Photographs on pages 76, 77, 98, 104, 105, 110
and 159 were provided by Wilborn & Associates,
Kansas City. www.wilbornfoto.com**

Printed in the United States of America
by Walsworth Publishing Co., Inc., Marceline, Mo.

To order copies, call StarInfo, 816-234-4636 (say
"Operator"). Or go to www.TheKansasCityStore.com

KANSAS CITY STAR BOOKS

TABLE OF CONTENTS

DEDICATION

For Debra, Charlie, Jessica and Sam: thanks for the noisy house.
— Brian Burnes

To the memories of Isaac and Michael Katz.
Their legacy of achievement, gratitude and generosity has endowed
all of us, their descendents, and for that we shall be eternally grateful.
— The Katz family

IT HAS OFTEN BEEN SAID that "Retail is Theatre." No one understood that better than Ike and his brother Mike Katz!

They combined retail dramatics with early Sam Walton pricing ideas.

Katz Drugs built its fame with "Katz Pays the Tax" on cigarettes, twofer pricing, promoting specials on tickets for the Kansas City Philharmonic and selling a defenseless teddy bear in defiance of the "Blue Law," which forbade selling non-necessities on Sundays.

I remember how Ike delighted in tossing little boxes of Beechies gum and other goodies from the second story patio of the Hollywood Beach Hotel in Hollywood, Florida, where our two families happened to be vacationing. My two brothers and I looked up with curiosity when we heard the "pop, pop, pops" of Ike's chewing gum, and saw our treasures falling toward us.

The two families had some similarities. My grandfather, Morris Helzberg, opened his first diamond shop in Kansas City, Kansas, in 1915. That was a year after Ike Katz had opened his first tobacco and confectionery store in downtown Kansas City, Missouri. The sons of immigrants, they both learned their business through trial and error, and both were inspired risk-takers whose belief in themselves was tested.

Both families began the Great Depression by expanding while other retailers were retrenching and just trying to hang on to what they had. In 1930, Ike added two more stores to the two he already owned in downtown Kansas City. My dad, Barnett C. Helzberg, Sr., had taken over the family business at age 15 when my grandfather had a stroke. During the Depression, he doubled the space of his flagship 11th and Walnut store, and remodeled with a grand flourish.

Both Ike and Dad had brothers with whom they formed business partnerships – Ike with his younger brother Mike, and my dad with his older brother Gilbert.

As a retailer, Dad respected Ike as a "Barnum," referring to the great American showman and later legislator P.T. Barnum, who was sometimes called the first show business millionaire. Like Barnum, nobody would forget Ike Katz.

Two unusual transactions highlighted our families' relationships.

Ike and Mike Katz had built a store on a 99-year, $1,000-per-month ground lease at 7th and Minnesota in Kansas City, Kansas. When Katz moved to 10th and Minnesota, Dad asked Ike if he could take over the ground lease. It was agreed and a Helzberg store was built there.

In turn, the new Katz store built at 10th and Minnesota was leased by Cousins Realty Company, a partnering of my brothers, Charles and Richard, and me, and Elaine and Suzanne Feld, daughters of our mother's cousin, Milton Feld.

When the Helzberg store at 7th and Minnesota closed, my brother Charles arranged to give it to the Archdiocese of Kansas City, Kansas.

Katz Drugs is a meaningful part of Kansas City history as well as an exciting and inspiring example of great retailing for all young entrepreneurs to be!

— Barnett C. Helzberg, Jr.

THE SPECIAL IMPORTANCE of being a grandfather became apparent to me a decade ago when I first became one myself. I'm fortunate to see my six grandchildren on a regular basis. Each calls me "poppy."

My earliest memories of my grandparents, Ike and Mama Minnie, were of visits to their home on Drury Lane in Kansas City. Ike would balance me on his knee, nuzzle me with his unshaven chin smelling of cigars, and sing either "Roll Out the Barrel" or "Let Me Call You Sweetheart." When he finished, he would straighten his leg, sending me tumbling to the floor. The home, with its swimming pool, tennis court and pool table, was a center of family activity. The entire group, Ike and Minnie's four married children, and 12 grandchildren, would gather there each spring to celebrate Passover.

I was fascinated by the collection of ornate canes in the front hallway. Grandpa had been crippled in a childhood accident and always walked with a cane. Neither grandparent ever drove a car.

My Father, Earl Katz, served in the Army Air Corps in WW II, and at one point was stationed in Salt Lake City, Utah. When I was about 7 or 8, Grandpa took me by train to Salt Lake to visit him. When we arrived at our hotel Grandpa had no idea what to do with his young grandson. His background selling newspapers gave him the idea to buy all the newspapers from the newsboy at the hotel in exchange for the young man taking me to the movies.

When I became a teenager, a special trip on Saturdays was riding the street car from Brookside to the downtown Katz office in the Boley Building for lunch with Dad and Grandpa on the Katz balcony. Grandpa and Dad shared an office that was always filled with cigar smoke; Grandpa had a brass spittoon by his desk. The walls were covered with photos of Grandpa and famous people like Jack Dempsey. And there were sayings, such as "I complained because I had no shoes until I met a man who had no feet."

Grandpa had a special friendship with Johnnie Dukie, the Kansas City Star newsboy who worked the street corner in front of the building. Johnnie wore leg braces from polio, and Grandpa had a standing order that the office buy most of his newspapers.

At age 14, I worked at the Katz Store at 39th and Main. Grandpa would always "hold court" at the store on Saturdays, and asked me to follow discretely behind customers with coupons, to see if they bought other things. I recall how proud I was that Grandpa asked me to do something so important to the business.

I left for college in 1953 and Katz Drugs observed its 40th anniversary in 1954. I recall on each visit home from school my parents insisted I visit my grandparents. "They won't be around forever," they would remind me. Grandpa and Mama Minnie lived at the Bellerive Hotel on East Armour Boulevard by then, and I regret I didn't follow my parents' advice more often. I traveled in Europe the summer of 1956, returned home unexpectedly, and found that Mama Minnie had passed away. Heartbroken, Grandpa moved in with us for a short time and passed away several months later in November.

It wasn't until years later that I realized my Grandfather's legacy. After his death, I graduated Dartmouth College in the class of 1957, and served a brief stint in the Air Force Reserve before joining the Katz Drug Company.

During my decade there I saw the company try to adjust to the self-service trends in the industry — which were contrary to the customer service business that had been nurtured by Ike and Mike, his brother and lifelong business partner. In my last years at Katz I was assigned to supervise a new plan in which the company opened leased depart-ments in the Woolco Discount Stores. Katz didn't thrive in this new "big box store" climate. I left for another career in 1969, and the company was sold to Skaggs in 1971.

Family and friends often suggested some-one should write a story about Ike, Mike, and the Katz Drug Company. I realized how little I knew of my Grandfather's history. I didn't know where he had come from, or when. Yet he was a legend in retailing and in the community. In 1965 Katz Hall, named after Isaac and Michael, was built at the University of Missouri Kansas City to house the UMKC School of Pharmacy.

In the early 1980's, genealogy became popular and helpful records like the early census results became available. I contacted family in St. Paul where Ike had lived from age 13. I was able over the next 25 years to research the family history, and perceive the thread that ran through Grandpa's life: his knack for seeing each challenge in life and business as an opportunity. On occasion I heard him say his crippled foot kept him from playing sports. So he focused his atten-tion and energy on business. Here is the story of challenges that became opportunities.

— Steve Katz

SELLING NEWSPAPERS

ON·THE·GREAT

NORTHERN RAILWAY

✦ 1893-1901 ✦

HOW IT ALL BEGAN

When Fetel and Sarah Katz immigrated with their children to the U.S., it set in motion one of the great, improbable American success stories. But first there were dues to be paid.

BEFORE the Katz Drug store empire, before the grinning neon cat, there was Fetel who married Sarah in about 1860 in the Ukrainian district known as the Pale.

Fetel and Sarah are the most distant ancestors that contemporary Katz family members have been able to identify. They had seven children: Hersh Ber, born in 1863; Victor, 1864; Sarah, 1868; Jennie, 1874; Isaac, 1879; Anne, 1884 and Michael in 1888.

Fetel probably traveled as a young man between his birthplace in Kopychyntsi, and Husiatyn, a trading center that was the site of a large synagogue, where he may have studied the Talmud.

As for the Pale, that was the district in Russia known as the Pale of Settlement, an area that at one time covered some 386,000 square miles between the Baltic and Black seas. From the 1770s through the early 1900s most Jews were required to live and work in the Pale.

Although restrictions on Jewish settlement were relaxed in the 1850s under Alexander II, the next czar, Alexander III, issued the Temporary Laws, which prohibited new Jewish settlements outside the Pale and allowed gentiles to expel Jews from their homes within the Pale. The mob violence of the pogroms followed in the early 1880s.

By then, Fetel and Sarah likely realized there was little future for Jews in the Pale. In 1888, the same year his youngest child was born, Fetel emigrated to

1800s

CIRCA 1860

Frank "Fetel" Katz marries Sara Hoffrichter in the Ukraine.

1878

Union Depot opens in Kansas City's West Bottoms district.

1879

Isaac Katz is born in Husiatyn, Ukraine.

1888

Michael Katz is born in Husiatyn, Ukraine.

Jewish life in the shtetls, or little towns, of the Pale was hard by design. The territory was created by Catherine the Great to force Jews from Imperial Russia, unless they converted to Orthodox Christianity.

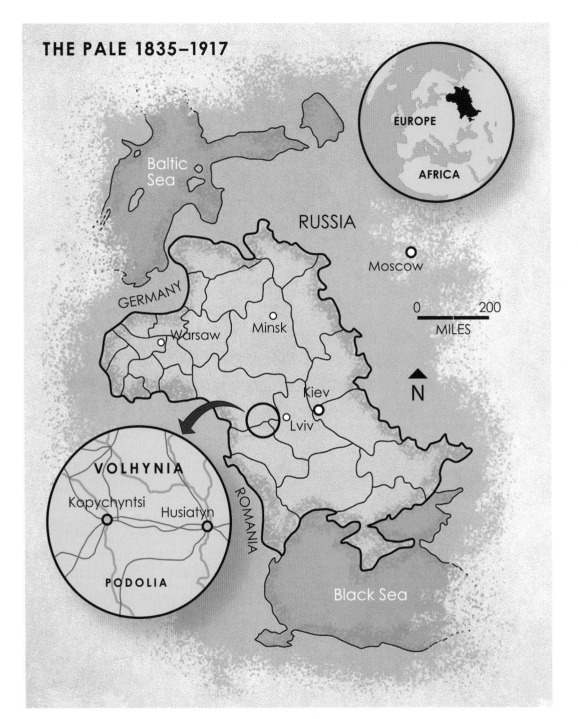

THE PALE 1835–1917

EUROPE
AFRICA

Baltic Sea

RUSSIA

Moscow

GERMANY

Warsaw

Minsk

0   200
MILES

N

Kiev

Lviv

VOLHYNIA

Kopychyntsi   Husiatyn

ROMANIA

PODOLIA

Black Sea

St. Paul, Minnesota. It's unclear why he chose St. Paul. It's possible the letters of earlier emigrants to the United States played a role in leading him there.

Sarah's surname had been Hoffrichter. Fetel's last name was not Katz, at least not in the Ukraine. At the time, many Jewish families had no surnames, going instead by "Solomon from Mintz," or "Benjamin son of David."

Steve Katz, a great-grandson of Fetel, believes that his great-grandfather probably took the name Katz as a contraction of *kohen*, which signifies membership in a priestly tribe, and *tzedek*, a Hebrew word for justice. The name would have roughly translated as "righteous priest."

FIRST STOP IN AMERICA

So it was Frank "Fetel" Katz who arrived in St. Paul in 1888, with the rest of the family — including Isaac, then 13 — following in 1892.

The family's address in St. Paul was 229 E. Indiana — within walking distance of the yards of the

Fetel preceded Sarah and their family in America by four years, a common practice in emigrating families.

1893

Isaac Katz begins selling newspapers on the Great Northern Railway.

1896

Klondike Gold Rush; Isaac Katz sells straw mats to gold seekers traveling west.

Isaac started — just as he had in St. Paul — by riding trains for a news company, selling newspapers.

Great Northern Railway, which in 1893 completed the northernmost transcontinental railroad route in the United States.

In 1893 Isaac turned 14 years old. That same year he took his first real job, selling newspapers on the railway.

If business was good, it grew only more so in 1896 with the discovery of gold in the Klondike River in Canada's Yukon Territory. And the best way west was on the Great Northern, on whose passenger cars Isaac by then was selling postcards, souvenirs, even Navajo blankets.

There was another item: straw mattresses. These appealed to the gold seekers whose train tickets assigned them spartan, often cushionless berths. Isaac sold the straw mattresses for $1.50 each. At the end of the line, according to Katz family legend, some passengers kept the straw mats while others left them on the train.

Isaac and other news vendors, or "butchers," arranged to have those mats shipped back to St. Paul to be sold again. According to one version of the story, Isaac lost his job when some of the railway officials didn't like the scheme.

But with some bad luck came some good. During his years on the Great Northern, Isaac had to navigate the rolling cars on a foot hobbled by an injury suffered during a baseball game. At about the turn of the century, he traveled to Chicago for surgery, taking with him $300.

When he got there, Isaac discovered the surgeon was away in Europe. But the setback proved a blessing, a pattern that would repeat itself throughout Isaac's early years. While staying in Chicago with a friend from St. Paul, Isaac was reintroduced to a former school mate, Minnie Baranov, whom he would marry in 1901.

Standing behind Frank and Sarah
in this handsome family portrait are
(from left) Michael, Anne, Sarah, Isaac,
Jennie, Victor and Hersh Ber.

Decades later (opposite page, right to left), Isaac, Michael, Isaac's son, Earl, and other Katz execs observe the ribbon-cutting at a new store.

His professional prospects in St. Paul seemed slim, and a friend suggested he try selling on the railroads out of Kansas City.

Isaac and Minnie moved to Kansas City in 1901. That would have placed them there in May, 1903, when the West Bottoms district — site of Union Depot — endured a ruinous flood. The depot itself was inundated.

Still, Isaac decided to stick with selling to railroad passengers.

He started — just as he had in St. Paul — by riding trains for a news company, selling newspapers. According to one account, Isaac's income of about $15 a week was a step down from his gold rush days, and he couldn't admit that to his wife. From his savings, which at this point totaled about $200, he took $5 each week to add to the pay envelope he handed to Minnie.

This allowed him to save face, at least until he got the idea of open-ing a fruit stand on Union Avenue, near the depot. He found a spot in the entrance of a hotel. Then, according to one account, Isaac discovered that Minnie had secretly saved more money than he had been taking out of his savings.

The fruit stand was the first Katz retail operation. Soon, Isaac sent to St. Paul for his younger brother, Michael, and they began what would become an inseparable partnership. They stocked fruit, as well as candy, postcards and souvenirs, merchan-dise not much different from what Isaac sold to the gold rushers some 10 years before.

LOW PRICES, HIGH VOLUME
Decades later, when the Katz brothers were opening new stores in Sioux City or Oklahoma City, they were interviewed by reporters from the local news-paper and obliged to tell the story of their success.

(Continued on page 27)

UNION DEPOT: GRAND STATION FOR A GRAND AMBITION

IT'S EASY TO IMAGINE Isaac Katz being pleased at his first glimpse of Union Depot when he visited Kansas City on the advice of a Chicago friend.

It had opened in the West Bottoms in 1878. That was less than 10 years after the completion of the Hannibal Bridge over the Missouri River connected Kansas City to markets in St. Louis, Chicago and New York.

Because of the depot's strategic location, Kansas City's founders were confident their city would play a growing national role as a rail center —and they wanted a station that reflected that.

"Handsomest and Largest Railroad Depot West of New York," read one headline on opening day, April 7, 1878. The red-brick building with its arched windows and 125-foot four-sided clock tower struck some as too ambi-

tious for Kansas City. But officials found it necessary to expand the building only two years later.

By 1888, the station boasted five direct routes to Denver and six to Chicago.

Isaac had lost his job on the Great Northern Railway, which he had ridden out of St. Paul. So in 1901 he and Minnie left for Kansas City, where he began again riding trains and selling newspapers. Two years later, a devastating flood convinced city leaders to consider building a new station well away from the low-lying West Bottoms.

The new Union Station opened in 1914, and Union Depot was demolished the next year. Today, the old depot's doorway stone, reading "Union Depot 1877," is on display in a Union Station concourse, the only remaining relic of Kansas City's first grand train station.

Finished in 1878 for $410,028, Union Depot had steeples, towers, turrets, arches, cupolas and detailed ornamentation. Critics reportedly referred to it as a "sprawling monstrosity" or "Kansas City's Insane Asylum."

This 1900 photograph of Kansas City's West Bottoms
was shot looking north along Union Avenue,
where a few years later Isaac Katz would open
his first fruit stand.

V-1459- Union Ave. (1900)

AT HIS FRUIT STAND ISAAC REALIZED THAT WHEN HIS COMPETITORS SOLD APPLES FOR 5 CENTS EACH, HE COULD ADVERTISE THREE APPLES FOR A DIME AND ATTRACT QUITE A FEW CUSTOMERS WHO WERE LOOKING FOR VALUE.

(Continued from page 22)

In the stories they wrote, the reporters routinely invoked Horatio Alger Jr., the Gilded Age author whose juvenile novels detailed how the humble could rise to riches through hard work. That indeed described the Katz brothers — Michael's first job in St. Paul was shining shoes. But the newspaper stories didn't always mention the 10 years the brothers labored before establishing their first two drug stores. Their success would not be the "eureka" moment of gold-rush legend, but a steady series of retail discoveries and innovations that allowed them ultimately to redefine "drug store."

They liked to tell the reporters about Isaac's discovery of competitive pricing — the most basic of retail concepts. At his fruit stand Isaac realized that when his competitors sold apples for 5 cents each,

he could advertise three apples for a dime and attract quite a few customers who were looking for value.

Sometimes the story was about oranges, not apples. But making money by charging low prices for high volume was something the brothers would remember when they opened two stores in downtown Kansas City.

A CENTURY LATER, A TRIP HOME

In 1999, Steve Katz, with his brother Ward, Ward's wife Donna, and Steve's oldest daughter, Jennifer Krause, visited the Ukraine, the home of Fetel and Sarah.

They went to the towns of Kopychyntsi and Husiatyn, hoping to find evidence of the family. Not only did they not find any clues, they found no evidence that there ever had been any Jewish life in the district.

"There was no trace," Katz said.

A FLOOD AND AN AUSPICIOUS MOVE TO HIGHER GROUND

ISAAC AND MINNIE KATZ apparently weren't personally affected by the flood that devastated the industrial neighborhoods of the West Bottoms in late May, 1903.

Others weren't so lucky. High water from the Kansas River spilled into the Kansas City, Kansas, districts of Argentine and Armourdale. Twenty people died. The high water swept away 16 of the 17 bridges that spanned the Kansas River in that area. One of the failed bridges had supported a water main that delivered fresh water to Kansas City, Missouri. For the next several days, speculators sold spring water for five cents a gallon. Fire officials prohibited the use of gasoline or kerosene for illumination.

As a result, The Kansas City Star reported, the city was left in "virtual darkness."

Some of the approximately 20,000 left homeless climbed the bluffs to seek shelter in Convention Hall, the city's grand hall re-built after a fire only three years before. Now it served as an aid station.

Isaac Katz probably was more concerned about a separate Kansas City showpiece, Union Depot. The flood left perhaps six feet of standing water in the station's interior. No trains ran for several days, something that would have affected Isaac the rail salesman, directly. Some 8,000 freight cars were submerged.

Yet Isaac remained, and prospered. In 1905 the Kansas City directory listed him as operator of a fruit stand at 1032 Union Avenue in the Bottoms. The next year's directory listed him with that fruit stand as well as a confectionery down the block at 1074 Union Avenue.

The 1908 directory again reported the 1032 Union Avenue address under Isaac's name, but this time identified his business as a hotel. By then the directory also was listing Michael Katz, who had been summoned from St. Paul by his brother.

The flood prompted a more focused dialogue in Kansas City about the location

---

Hardest hit in the 1903 flood were the rail and stockyards of the West Bottoms.

SOUTH
VENUE.
EPOT
EFT

A FLOOD (CONTINUED)

of any new train station. While some had advocated a West Bottoms location, the high water in 1903 killed that option. A different, less flood-prone location would secure the city's position as the country's second-largest rail center behind Chicago.

It also would eliminate the seedy district that surrounded Union Depot. For years, many travelers' first sight of Kansas City had been of tacky urban density, including saloons and brothels. The new Union Station opened south of downtown in 1914. Union Depot was demolished the following year, and the area's saloon owners and madams began to disperse.

Among those leaving for higher ground were the Katz brothers.

CIGARETTES

TZ DAYS THE I

WORLD WAR I: THE OPPORTUNITY OF A LIFETIME

With the country at war, the government placed a tax on cigarettes, and ordered retail stores to close early to save fuel — not good news for small business. Or was it?

IT WAS 1917, and Michael Katz was taking a walk around downtown Kansas City.

The U.S. had entered World War I and the government had just instituted a one-cent wartime tax on cigarettes. Michael and his brother Isaac operated two downtown Kansas City stores. The city directory listed them under the title "confectionery."

But they also sold tobacco. Individual packs of cigarettes were 10 cents each. A one-cent increase represented a significant jump.

The brothers had opened the two stores in 1914, the first at 12th and McGee streets, on the first floor of the Renaissance Revival-style Argyle Building, and the second store at 8th Street and Grand Avenue.

While business was steady, it was hardly making them rich. They already worked 19-hour days. And anything that threatened to upset the delicate balance of costs and revenue was no small thing.

On his walk, Katz noticed that other stores simply had passed the cigarette tax along to their customers. Some had done more than that, using the tax as an opportunity to make a little more money by charging 25 cents for two packs of cigarettes. Some simply increased the price of a single pack to 15 cents.

It was as if the retailers couldn't be bothered with pennies. But the Katz brothers had learned down on Union Avenue the magic of a penny not charged.

1914

Isaac and
Michael Katz
open their first
store at 12th and
McGee, then a
second location
at 8th and Grand.

1917

United States
declares war on
Germany; federal
government
requires all retail
stores, except
pharmacies, to
close at 6 p.m.

1917

After the U.S.
government
imposes a one-
cent tax on packs
of cigarettes, Katz
brothers discount
the one-cent tax
and advertise that
"Katz Pays the Tax."

**The Katz logo
went on every
pack of
cigarettes
they handled.**

They decided not to raise the price at all. They would cover it. In their store windows they placed signs that read: "Cigarettes same old price — Katz Pays the Tax."

FAST NICKELS

"It struck the psychology of the moment," wrote Kansas City Star staff writer Richard B. Fowler in 1933. "The store was crowded. The cigarettes were sold as fast as the clerks could hand them across the counters, at a profit of a half-cent per pack."

"Fast nickels are better than slow dimes," Isaac liked to say.

The price attracted not only customers but other retailers, who bought in bulk from Katz and then placed the packs of cigarettes on their own shelves. This prompted Isaac Katz to devise a small branding iron that imprinted the packs with the Katz logo, identify-ing to all the source of the cheap cigarettes. Business was so brisk, according to one Katz legend, that the brothers installed metal cash register drawers to replace the wooden ones that wore out.

Not surprisingly, they encoun-tered immediate headwinds when word got around regarding their per-pack price.

According to the Fowler ver-sion, they were called on the carpet by tobacco suppliers for "ruining" the Kansas City cigarette market by undercutting the other mer-chants who had passed on the tax to their customers. The operator of a tobacco store chain warned the Katz brothers that they would be put out of the cigarette business in Kansas City.

The brothers insisted that they were small-time operators who had managed to lay in a large inven-tory of cigarettes at a one-time low

1920s

1920

Prohibition of liquor takes effect; the 18th Amendment was ratified in 1919.

1921

Isaac and Minnie move to 3629 Harrison Blvd. in the stylish Hyde Park district of Kansas City.

1923

The first retail building opens in the new Country Club Plaza shopping district.

1929

The Katz drug chain goes public one month before the stock market crashes.

In the right ad writer's hands, a matchbook is as good as a billboard.

wholesale price, and they had no designs on upsetting the Kansas City tobacco market.

That bought them some time, Fowler wrote. In the meantime, they had learned the wisdom of advertising. "Katz Pays the Tax" set them apart from the more than 120 other confectioneries listed in the 1917 Kansas City directory. So when a sales representative from The Kansas City Star came by to ask for their business, they were ready. For the next six decades, Katz would be among the newspaper's biggest advertisers.

According to Katz family members, the government eventually intervened in the "Katz Pays the Tax" campaign, enjoining the stores from using the slogan. But a photograph of the Argyle Building taken in 1925 — some seven years after Armistice Day — shows the slogan still displayed on the store's exterior signage.

Ike and Mike opened their Argyle Building store at 12th and McGee, in 1914. It was, fortuitously, in a building full of doctors.

The Katz confectioneries became drug stores but kept the banana splits.

YOU WANT A PHARMACY ...?

History provided another opening for the brothers to exercise their risk-taking smarts.

There was no shortage of drug stores in Kansas City. In 1901, when Isaac Katz arrived, the directory listed more than 150 of them.

But in 1917 Federal administrators ordered all retail stores to close at 6 p.m. to help save fuel in war time — except pharmacies, which were exempted from the rule. The brothers knew that a 6 p.m. closing time for their confectioneries would mean losing the small daily spike in tobacco sales that occurred as downtown office workers headed home.

The Katz confectioneries became drug stores.

Almost immediately, according to one version of the story, a representative of the Federal Food Administration came by the 12th and McGee store to inquire about the new status. Isaac Katz directed him to a back room, behind the tobacco, the candy and the small soda fountain.

In the '20s, Katz and other pharmacists filled prescriptions for "medicines" that were whiskey in disguise.

"There on the floor in a more or less disorderly condition, was a collection of pills, powders and patent medicines, enough to stock a small but actual drug store," read the unidentified news story. The investigator was introduced to the staff pharmacist — recently hired for $22 a week — and that was how the Katz brothers began the first day of the Katz Drug store. They had already sold $5.73 of medications when the feds arrived.

If the Katz brothers hired proper pharmacists, they also stocked over-the-counter patent medicines or folk remedies, such as the herbal compounds marketed by entrepreneur Lydia Pinkham for menstrual pains, the Swamproot line of pills and ointments, and an alcohol-based nostrum called Peruna.

Isaac bought these items in bulk from a wholesale supplier and put them on his shelves. But he thought they didn't move fast enough. "After a time he got tired of looking at these packages," Lewis Jay Navran, a Katz executive in the 1930s, wrote in an undated memoir.

THE BROTHERS INSISTED THAT THEY WERE SMALL-TIME OPERATORS WHO HAD MANAGED TO LAY IN A LARGE INVENTORY OF CIGARETTES AT A ONE-TIME LOW PRICE.

In those days, Navran wrote, a drug store paid 50 cents for such medicines that retailed for one dollar. No one had thought about cutting the prices. But Isaac decided

A 1914 picture of the tobacco counter at the new Katz store at 8th and Grand shows friendly staff and bargains of the day.

One day Ike read in the paper that only pharmacies would be allowed to stay open past 6 p.m. The next day he turned the brothers' confectionery at 8th and Grand into a drug store. This 1920 photograph shows the store's location on a busy trolley car stop.

to mark them down. "The results were astonishing," Navran wrote, prompting "a whole flock of customers coming into the Katz brothers' operation."

Thus three things — the cigarette tax, advertising, and the 6 p.m. closing time — came together to create a tipping point that had big ramifications for the brothers' business.

The story about how the brothers came to open that first downtown store underscores the meeting of intuition and luck that marked their early years.

It goes that Isaac was out with Minnie when he strode into a tobacco and candy store at 12th and McGee, liked the sight of it and announced he was going to buy it.

It's hard to imagine Isaac Katz, who had been carefully building up his business equity over 10 years along Union Avenue, being that cavalier about any new location. A closer reading suggests that both brothers had noticed the streetcar tracks outside the store and the constant foot traffic that passed its front door.

They found a second location at 8th Street and Grand Avenue.

BUSINESS WEEK BELIEVED THE NIRA'S PRICE FIXING PROVISIONS HAD BEEN AIMED SPECIFICALLY AT KATZ.

The proprietor told them that the store wasn't for sale. As they later learned, he was behind in his rent and would soon be put out by the owner. Not much time passed before the Katz brothers were installed at the location.

ROLL OUT THE BARREL
Finally, as a business-booster, it's hard to ignore the salutary effect of Prohibition.
(Continued on page 47)

Katz brand pure powdered sulphur was used as a medicinal tonic and laxative.

The Katz mail order catalog offered more than 25,000 items, one-day service, and a money-back guarantee. Take that Sears, Roebuck!

SEE THAT PROTECTIVE METAL CAP IS STENCILED
"KENTUCKY TAVERN"
IN BOND
Katz
DRUG CO.
PHONES: BE. 1701-1702
KANSAS CITY
CHECKED BY NO
Katz
Drug Company
12th and Walnut Sts.
— Phone —
KANSAS CITY, MO.
No.
Dr.
Serial No.
Kind
Quantity
Proof
Patient's Name
Directions
Date Canceled
NCTURE BENZOIN
CERTIFIED
CONTROLLED SUBSTANCE RX
NAME
ADDRESS
Doctor
Address
BLUE STEEL
BLADES
DOUBLE EDGE
Katz
THE
KATZ PERFECT
MENTHOL INHALER
MADE OF
PURE MENTHOL CRYSTAL
Total
Purchased
% of Sales 13% Plus
244,755.32
266,400.71
ESTIMATED PROFIT

(Continued from page 43)

After it became the law of the land in January 1920, the Katz brothers benefited — as did all pharmacy owners — from the widespread practice of doctors prescribing alcohol to patients for "medicinal" purposes.

In reality, Kansas City authorities operating under Pendergast machine rule often chose to overlook liquor infractions. In the '20s and early '30s the city's signature jazz sound emanated from any number of nightclubs, many operating illegally. Case in point: During the Depression, Kansas City was one place where a musician could reliably find work.

Authorities would make the occasional show of draining large barrels of whiskey into the street or river, and busting up home distilleries.

Broadcast news icon Walter Cronkite, who spent much of his youth in Kansas City, remembered a raid on a residence only a couple of doors down from his.

His mother, he once wrote, "watched with horror and I with

U.S. marshals dump five barrels of Jamaica ginger extract into the Missouri River in this 1931 photo.

Katz Drug Co.

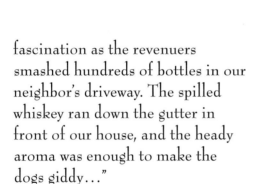

This solid brass mortar and pestle sat in a Katz pharmacy.

fascination as the revenuers smashed hundreds of bottles in our neighbor's driveway. The spilled whiskey ran down the gutter in front of our house, and the heady aroma was enough to make the dogs giddy…"

Even in Kansas City, there was plenty of work for those charged with enforcing the national ban on alcohol — sometimes referred to as the Noble Experiment. In 1922 Congress approved legislation establishing 20 more federal judges, including one for the Western District of Missouri, which included Kansas

City, in part because of the case load generated by liquor violations.

However the topic sometimes seemed more a source of mirth, even for federal judges. Merrill E. Otis, faced with the high number of cases involving small speakeasies and home distillery operators, once said he scheduled such cases at night "on the theory that it is

appropriate to try them when the moon shines."

Baltimore writer H. L. Mencken, covering the 1928 Republican National Convention in Kansas City, interviewed two African-American Republican delegates among those gathering in Convention Hall.

"They have remained the most intelligent men I have encountered among persons officially attached to the convention, one United States senator and five bootleggers excepted," Mencken wrote in an article reprinted in The Kansas City Star. *(Continued on page 53)*

Katz BROADCASTER

Issued by Katz Drug Company   Prices Herein Listed are Good Until July 1, 1928.   SPRING 1928.

AMAZING BARGAINS FOR EVERYBODY
Katz CUTS PRICES TO ROCK BOTTOM!

Read What Your Friends Say:

I always have had good service from Katz. I like to deal with you.
Mrs. Morrill A. Young, Scranton, Kas.

I have ordered goods from you several times in the past few years and every article was entirely satisfactory.
F. E. Tarpy, RFD 1, Pawnee Rock, Kas.

You have always been very prompt in taking care of us.
John R. Key, Carthage, Mo.

Thanking you for the prompt service. Your merchandise has always given me great satisfaction.
F. L. Esringer.

I am an old customer and a real satisfied one.
Mrs. Grace Boswell, Penalosa, Kansas.

I have sent you four orders this winter and everything has been satisfactory. Yours for good drugs cheaper,
O. B. Gentry.

I wish to thank you very kindly for your courtesy in adjusting this matter. When I came out to this country in 1925, no one in Oberlin had ever heard of the Katz Drug Company. By referring several of my patients to your concern you have established quite a business out here.
Dr. ___ ___, Oberlin, Kansas

Please find enclosed my check for one box of Dutch Masters Cigars. I was very well pleased with the cigars I bought of you last month. I am
O. J. Keuper, M.D., Chamois, Mo.

Excuse me for sending two orders in same week, you shouldn't have so many bargains.
G. V. Redford, Holden, Mo.

I'm used to getting so much for my money at Katz.
Mrs. W. A. Scidmore, Texcott, Kansas.

It Must Be as Good as We Say It Is---

Our Reputation and Responsibility Is Your Strongest Guarantee

Friends in bringing the great Katz Drug Stores to you—by mail—we have but one object in view!

That is to render the same efficient service on the same high quality merchandise as we do personally at our stores. We have built this enormous business of ours on Quality Merchandise at low prices. Our stores are crowded constantly with those seeking the greatest values that money can buy. These people know that Katz prices are Rock Bottom. The amount of business that we do is tremendous. It has to be—in order that we can sell at such amazingly low prices.

High quality and low prices go hand in hand at Katz. We carry only the highest class of standard advertised goods. We are sure that you will not be disappointed with anything that you buy from us.

Go over the items listed in this "Broadcaster" carefully. Select those that you need. Compare our prices with what you are paying now. Remember that during this sale ___ ___ paying the ___ ___ ___ saving is worth money to you to make up your order for all the merchandise that you can use now. This is really a big opportunity for you to save money.

We will appreciate it if you will tell your friends about the savings you make at our stores and send us their names.

If you do not see listed what you want—write in for prices as we carry over 25,000 items, all at Katz deep cut prices. Every article is guaranteed to be exactly as represented.

I. KATZ — M. H. KATZ
Owners and Operators
of the Katz Drug Stores

What It Means to You When Buying from Katz

A saving of 20 to 40 per cent on your purchases. Receiving just what you order as WE DO NOT SUBSTITUTE. Obtaining only standard and Nationally advertised brands of merchandise.

The enormous business of the Katz Drug Company was ___ of selling EVERYTH___ attaining the phenom___ ing 5 Million Dolla___ Company has to o___ received. Linked h___ great savings offere___ and satisfaction. It ___ say it is. The na___ known throughout ___ OUR REPUTATIO___ GUARD. If for an___ satisfied with your ___ liberty to return ___ your money will be ___ bank or wholesale ___ bility of the Katz D___

Ours is more tha___ carry over 25,000 ___ partments, such as ___ Goods, Cutlery, El___ dries, Household Ne___ Rubber Goods, and ___ ments in addition ___ and Drug Sundries. ___ co-operate to the f___ you prices on anyth___

Our mail order ___ ped to give you pr___ tention. Our men a___ art of packing and ___ rest assured that y___ you in first class co___

Send in your ord___ of the many wonde___ and DON'T FORG___ Leading Cut Rate ___ EVERYTHING FOR ___

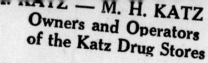

EVERYTHING FOR LESS

$1.20
...dwell's
...of Pepsin
6c

...ello Muscle
...... **$1.79**
...ello Motor
...... **43¢**
...ello Brillian-
...... **39¢**
...ello Acne
...... **48¢**
...nello Astrin-
...ion ...... **79¢**
...nello Tissue
...... **43¢**
...rinello Face
...... **39¢**

.00
S S
...emedy
19

...nello

...llo Lettuce
...... **79¢**

Powders

...ary Garden Face
... . **79¢**
... Peacock Tonic
... . **56¢**
...avis Face Pow-
... . **38¢**
...mpeian Face Pow-
... . **42¢**
...Melba Face Pow-
... . **39¢**
... Marsha Cream
...wder ...... **69¢**
...jer Kiss Face Pow-
... . **39¢**
...Carmen Face Pow-
... . **38¢**

Toiletries

...c Amami Bath Pow-
...der ...... **39¢**
...00 Coty's Single Com-
...pacts ...... **79¢**
...1.00 Djer Kiss Sachet
...Powder ...... **73¢**
...50c Melba Rouge ...... **39¢**
...$1.25 Mary Garden Toi-
...let Water ...... **97¢**
...$1.00 Newbros Quinine
...Hair Tonic ...... **79¢**
...35c Djer Kiss Talcum
...Powder ...... **21¢**
...$1.00 Tangee Lip
...stick ...... **78¢**

Houbigant

75c Houbigant Face Powder ...... **.69¢**
$1.00 Houbigant Ideal Talcum ...... **79¢**
$2 Houbigant Perfume ½ oz. **$1.79**
$1.75 Houbigant Ideal Vegetal **$1.49**
50c Houbigant Shaving Cream ...... **.39¢**
$3.50 Houbigant Toilet Water **$2.98**
$2.50 Houbigant Double Compacts **$2.09**
$6.75 Houbigant Ideal Perfume, 2 oz. **$5.89**

Perfumes

Imported and domestic perfumes packed in original packages.
$4.00 Coty's Perfume, 1 oz. **$3.19**
$2.00 Djer Kiss Perfume, 1 oz. **$1.49**
$7.00 Carons Black Narcissus **$5.69**
$10.00 Toujours Moi (Always Me) **$8.98**
$1.00 Houbigant Purse Size **86¢**
$2.00 Assorted Perfumes **$1.69**
$3.00 Cheramy Biarritz Perfume **$2.29**
$3.50 Houbigants Ideal Perfume, 1 oz. **$2.98**
$6.50 Coty's Paris Perfume 2 oz. **$4.98**
We carry a complete line of Rubenstein, Harriet Hubbard Ayres, Richard Hudnut and all other standard brands. Write for prices.

Van Ess Grows Hair

Van Ess liquid scalp massage scientifically massages the scalp. It works into the surface elements that kill germs and rejuvenates hair roots. Sold on positive money back guarantee. Regular $4.50 treatment of three bottles special **$2.98**

Hoppers

50c Hoppers Face Powder ...... **39¢**
60c Hoppers Cold Cream ...... **42¢**
75c Hoppers Wave & Sheen ...... **59¢**
50c Hoppers Hair Youth ...... **37¢**
60c Hoppers Fruity Shampoo ...... **48¢**
75c Hoppers Liquid Cleanser ...... **59¢**
60c Hoppers Vanishing Cream ...... **42¢**
50c Hoppers White Clay Tube ...... **39¢**

Face Creams

50c Melba Vanishing Cream ...... **39¢**
75c Princess Pat Skin Food ...... **56¢**
50c Pompeian Massage Cream ...... **38¢**
$1.00 Nadinola Bleach Cream ...... **78¢**
$1.00 Peacock Tissue Cream ...... **79¢**
$1.25 Othine for Bleaching ...... **84¢**
75c Boncilla Cold Cream ...... **54¢**
$1.00 Vivadou Astringent Cream **79¢**

Dentrifices

50c Pebeco Tooth Paste ...... **33¢**
60c Forhan's Tooth Paste ...... **41¢**
$1.00 Corego Plate Powder ...... **79¢**
50c Day Dream Tooth Paste ...... **33¢**
60c Lyons Tooth Powder ...... **43¢**
50c Iodent Tooth Paste ...... **38¢**
50c Ipana Tooth Paste ...... **37¢**
$1.00 Moore's Mouth Wash ...... **79¢**

FREE With every purchase of Williams shaving cream, a 2½ ounce bottle of Williams Aqua Velva Shaving Lotion. Extra Especial 60c value. All for ...... **29¢**

Narcissus Body Powder

An exceptionally high grade of body powder in an artistically designed metal container 1 Lb. can, with large Velour powder puff. Reg. $1.00. Special ...... **59¢**

FREE With every purchase of 75c box Melba Love Me Face powder, one 50c jar of Melba Cleansing Cream FREE. Reg. $1.25 value. Both for ...... **73¢**

65c Ponds Vanishing Cream 39c

$1.00 Mulsified Cocoanut Oil Shampoo Special 78c

$1.00 D. & R. Cold Cream 79c

35c Palm-Olive Shaving Cream 24c

50c Princess Pat Rouge Special 36c

Katz Drug Company
The Aristocrat of Almanacs
The North American Almanac
1927
The Worlds Leading Cut Rate Drug Stores
Katz
Pays the Tax
STEEL CUT
Season's Greetings from the Katz Drug Co.
LINEN FINISH
LINEN · FINISH
CAMERA DEPT.
PRESCRIPTION SPECIALISTS
10th & Minnesota
Kansas City, Kansas 64101
Doctor's Phone FI 2-4719
Katz
Parking Lot, 8th and Grand
TIME OUT
TIME IN
RAIN CHECK!
WE ARE TEMPORARILY OUT OF THE MERCHANDISE YOU REQUESTED AS ADVERTISED!
DRUG COMPANY

(Continued from page 48)

That same year the federal chief of Prohibition enforcement in Kansas City conceded that more speakeasies had opened in the city after Prohibition than legitimate bars had operated there before it.

On the home front, things were going well. In 1921, Ike and Minnie, now a family of six, moved to a stylish Hyde Park house at 3629 Harrison Blvd.

A BLUR OF CREATIVITY

Today it's easy imagining Isaac and Michael Katz walking downtown Kansas City streets during the 1920s.

It was a city of possibilities. St. Louis grew only 6.3 percent during that decade while Kansas City's population increased by 23.2 percent. The number of building permits increased 65 percent between 1915 and 1923.

Dreamers flourished there. Both *(Continued on page 56)*

An ad targets the desires of the day: health, a full head of hair, and nice glasses.

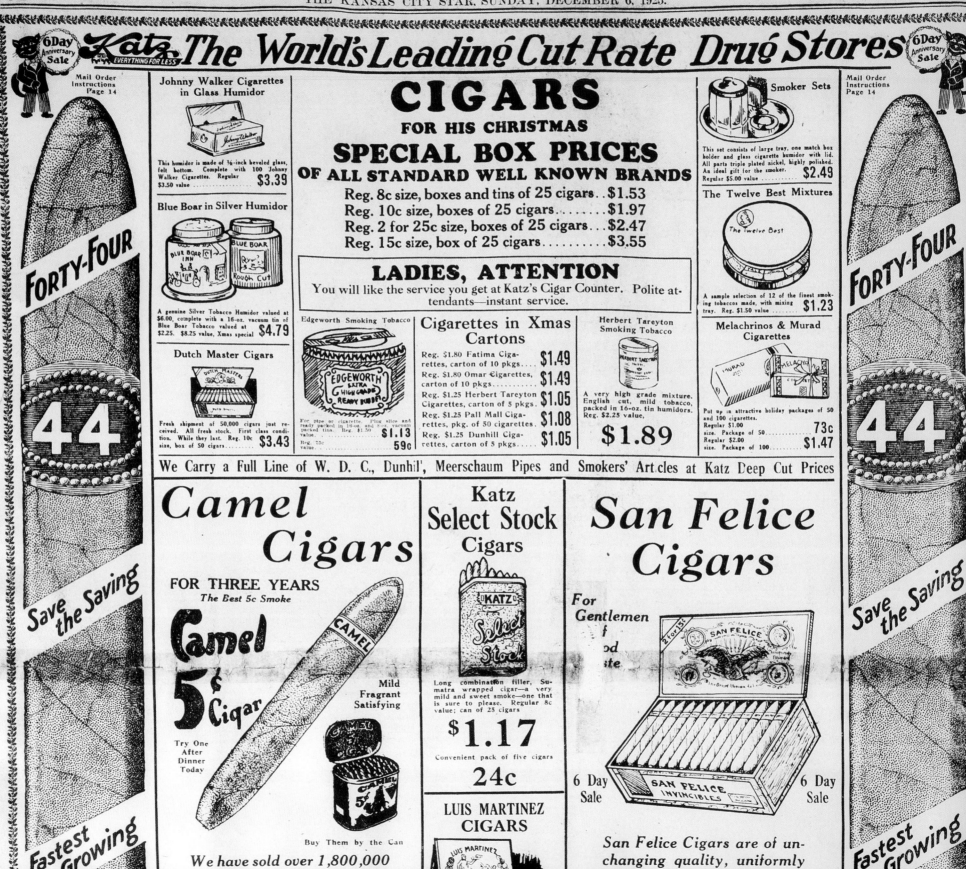

HERBERT HOOVER'S 'GIFT' TO THE KATZ BROTHERS

IT WAS HERBERT HOOVER, then U.S. Food Administration head, who issued the order that no tobacco shop or confectionery could remain open past 6 p.m., pharmacies excepted.

Isaac and Michael Katz, who read of the order in the morning paper, by that night had hired a pharmacist and set him up at their 12th and McGee Street store along with a small inventory of pharmaceuticals.

It helped that the downtown office building that included their store, the Argyle Building, was filled with doctors who wrote prescriptions for patients who then headed for the nearest pharmacy, which was the Katz drug store just downstairs. The Katz brothers soon hired a pharmacist for their other store at 8th Street and Grand Avenue.

Of course it wasn't Hoover who made a drug store of the Katz candy shop. It was the brothers' response to Hoover's order.

HERBERT HOOVER PRESIDENTIAL LIBRARY & MUSEUM

But they had to walk a careful line not to appear to ignore the food administration. Hoover, as head of the Commission for the Relief of Belgium in 1914, had helped that country's residents avoid starvation under German occupation. He considered food a weapon that could win World War I.

In that context, business owners ignored the edicts of the U.S. Food Administration at their peril. For instance, government officials advised that since wheat was the most important agricultural commodity to conserve, bakers should substitute corn or other grains whenever possible in producing bread. Those bakeries occasionally found in violation of these guidelines were closed for one day, two days or a week.

In 1918, eight bakeries in Kansas City were cited for such violations. Those bakeries donated $425 to the American Red Cross "in lieu of further prosecution."

(Continued from page 53)

A young artist named Walt Disney was part of the creative fervor in 1920s Kansas City. In 1946, he and his wife Lillian came back for a visit and Walt got a hero's welcome.

Walt Disney and Harry Truman suffered business reversals in early 1920s Kansas City; Disney's first animation company went bankrupt, and Truman shut down his downtown haberdashery. Neither was discouraged.

It was that kind of place. A reporter writing in the New Republic magazine in 1928 referred to Kansas City as a "city whose god is motion and whose ideal is change." In 1926 President Calvin Coolidge came to Kansas City to dedicate the completed Liberty Memorial, a monument

A REPORTER WRITING IN THE NEW REPUBLIC REFERRED TO KANSAS CITY AS A "CITY WHOSE GOD IS MOTION AND WHOSE IDEAL IS CHANGE."

to those who died in World War I. The next year city leaders persuaded Charles Lindbergh to dedicate their new airport.

Sinclair Lewis researched his 1927 novel *Elmer Gantry*, concerning an unprincipled preacher, in Kansas City.

The next year the Republican Party held its national convention in Kansas City, nominating Herbert Hoover, well-known to both Katz brothers, for president.

In 1929 the Katz brothers took their company public, issuing stock.

What could possibly go wrong?

THE UNITED STATES declared war on Germany in April 1917.

American troops began landing in France in June, the first of about two million Americans who would serve there. The first units entered trenches in October..

The mood in Kansas City was sufficiently charged and sobered.

"This is our first Christmas in the war," wrote J.C. Nichols, Kansas City real estate developer and area chairman of an American Red Cross membership campaign, on Dec. 23, 1917.

"It is a chance for every true American to enlist on the side of those who are actively defending him," Nichols was quoted in The Kansas City Star.

"We do not know what next Christmas will bring. Homes not yet

About This Photo

MILITARY **exercises, such as this one at Swope Park, were held across Kansas City.**

affected may have an empty chair at that time."

A year later, readers of The Star had grown used to the terrible shorthand used to describe the toll of battle. Over separate lists of names, the abbreviations "W. Sv.," "M.A." and "W. D. U." denoted those Kansas City area men who had been wounded severely, were missing in action, or had wounds the degree of which were still unknown.

Two nights a week in December 1917, Kansas City was lightless. A nationwide coal shortage compelled federal fuel administrators to announce that Sunday and Thursday nights should not be illuminated, to conserve electricity and the coal burned to help generate it.

Voluntary expressions of support may not have been all that voluntary. During the December 1917 American Red Cross nationwide membership

drive, citizens were asked to join for $1 and wear the button they had received.

At downtown intersections, speakers urged support for the campaign.

Boy Scout troops acted as roving compliance squads, knocking on individual doors to ask — politely, according to The Star — why there wasn't a Red Cross membership banner in the window.

Others were not so diplomatic. A written excuse from every employee who didn't join the Red Cross was required by the chief executive of the local Montgomery Ward & Co., The Star reported.

Missouri Governor Frederick Gardner supported efforts to eliminate the German language in the state, and the Missouri superintendent of schools refused to certify high schools that continued to teach German. The Council of Defense in Cass County, just south of Kansas City, prohibited the use of the German language over the telephone.

One high-profile case of perceived disloyalty involved a minister, the Rev. Louis J. Schwartz, pastor of the German Emanuel Evangelical Lutheran Church at 16th and Cherry streets. Schwartz had declined to promote "Baby Bonds," a government war security, during services, saying the pulpit was not the place for such an appeal. But some Missouri residents were more than willing at the time to suspend separation of church and state.

The chairman of the Kansas City Baby Bonds committee submitted a summary of the Schwartz matter to the local United States attorney. Ultimately, The Star reported, Rev. Schwartz demonstrated his loyalty at the conclusion of a service, when he asked departing church members to support the bond drive.

"All of my people are loyal Americans," he told The Star. "I doubt if more than five came from Germany. I have lived in Kansas City 25 years and am as patriotic as anyone."

WELCOMES IT'S EMPL...
YOUR PLACE IS WAITING FOR YO...

DRUG STORE
HUNTER BROS.
Open All Night.

HUNTER BROS.

CAR STOP

35TH DIV. 140TH INFANTRY K.C. Mo. MAY 10 1919

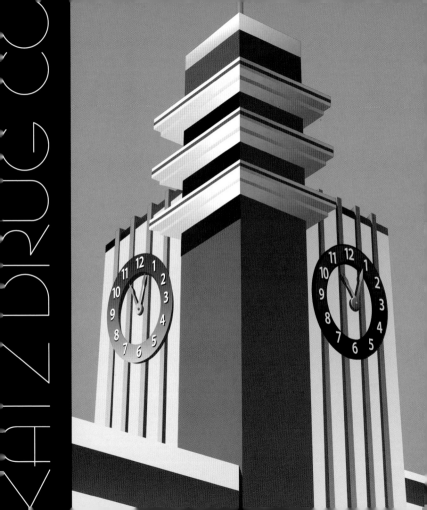

DEPRESSION, WHAT DEPRESSION?

Cash vanishes, but Katz hires architects and opens stores that make statements. It fields fleets of well-trained employees, and leads the trek to "suburbia."

THE STOCK MARKET CRASHED on October 29, 1929 (Black Tuesday) ushering in the Great Depression.

Americans watched, dumbstruck, as stock prices plummeted. Shareholders tried to unload their securities, but no one was buying. Banks heavily invested in the market were forced to close, and those failures spread panic across the country. Consumer spending virtually stopped, hiring stopped, businesses closed. Millions were out of work, and the devastation quickly spread to other countries.

In Missouri, the Depression was brutal. Unemployment was almost 16 percent in 1930, 27 percent in 1931 and more than 38 percent in 1932, when the national average was only 23.6 percent.

But somebody forgot to tell the Katz brothers of Kansas City that they were in the middle of the biggest economic and social collapse of the century.

Katz's newly issued stock did lose earnings-per-share — from $3.53 in 1929 to $2.74 in 1930. But by 1931 it had made up the loss, and then some. By 1934 per-share earnings stood at a record $4.75. The lucky ones who held it in late 1934 got a $3 dividend.

In 1930, while other merchants were closing stores, the brothers opened two, a 10th and Main Street store in Kansas City that April, and then a store in Des Moines. People were hard up and shopping for bargains. They opened two more in 1931,

Soup lines in cities and towns across the
country were a stark reminder of how close
to the bottom some Americans were.

198. The Boley Building, Kansas City, Mo.

Postcard scene of the 1908 Louis Curtiss-designed Boley Building shows five horse-drawn vehicles and street car tracks.

both in Kansas City, Mo. — one at 12th Street and Baltimore Avenue in January, and one at 12th and Walnut streets that October. The company's main offices were in the 12th and Walnut store, the Boley Building.

With their compounding prosperity, Ike and Minnie moved from Hyde Park onto what can only be called an estate.

It was on Drury Lane in what is now the elite, well-groomed incorporated city of Mission Hills.

Steve Katz remembers, "as if it were yesterday," that it had a swimming pool with water-spouting lions and a wading pool for children, a pond stocked with gold fish, an enormous greenhouse *(Continued on page 68)*

MEMORIES

Each Sunday my three friends and I would attend church, go to the movies, and then go to Katz's to have the limeades. At the time (the late 1950's) we would order the limeade and get to keep the glass. They were tall and dark green! I have eight in my cabinet today that I use for vodka tonics served with a slice of lime!

Carolyn White
Marblehead, Mass.

My husband and I bought a house in Roeland Park in July 1967, and the realtor suggested we meet at Katz drugstore there to sign the papers. We sat at the fountain. Katz was always a special place for us!
Rosemary Cole
Mission, Kan.

1930

Michael Katz is kidnapped; released after family pays a $100,000 ransom.

1932

Unemployment in Missouri stands at 38 percent (12.6 percent nationwide).

1932

First Katz "Million Dollar Sale" successfully generates $1 million in sales in one month.

1933

Prohibition repealed.

The Katz Drury Lane residence had curb appeal and (below, from left) a grand pool, a garden teahouse, and a pond and bridge (captured on glass negatives by Frank Lauder).

Rose and Michael Katz's home, designed by Kansas City architect Robert Gornall, had a massive stone-clad tower and a loggia with stone columns.

(Continued from page 65) and the first lighted tennis court in Kansas City. "Momma Minnie" was proud to show off her rose gardens.

Meanwhile, Isaac's brother and partner Michael Katz and his wife, Rose, had built an elaborately designed Tudor-style home on the city's grandest boulevard, Ward Parkway. Set on an expansive corner lot, with a tall, steeply pitched front gable, a recessed arched doorway and three massive chimneys topped by decorative chimney pots, it was hard to miss.

A KIDNAPPING THAT RIVETED THE CITY

Steve Katz believes that the public stock option and the family's growing wealth is exactly what attracted the mobsters who kidnapped Michael Katz for $100,000 ransom in 1930. The story had a happy ending but the monies were never recovered.

(A Katz store would become a footnote in another kidnapping, the 1953 abduction of young Bobby Greenlease, the son of a prominent Kansas City Cadillac dealer. The kidnappers used the

From the entrance wing of the Michael Katz residence, a grand staircase rose to four second-floor bedrooms, a nursery and four baths.

69

MEMORIES

Just the name of the Katz Drug Stores brings a smile to my face. Back then it was a special treat to go the distance to the store at 40th and Main and, if we were really lucky, we stopped by Velvet Creme for an ice cream cone. Life was much simpler then and it didn't take a whole lot to make us happy.

Jane Fisher McGinley Gladstone, Mo.

I definitely remember Katz Drugstore on Main Street in the Westport area. I was really upset when they took down the Katz head. What did they do with the cat heads? Hopefully they are somewhere being taken care of.

Nancy Crossfield Belton, Mo.

Today many Katz-branded products are collected for their nostalgia value, bought and sold on eBay and other collectors' sites. There's reason to believe this razor and case was produced as a holiday gift to doctors.

parking lot of the Katz store at Westport and Main as a rendezvous point. There they transferred the 6-year-old to the car used to drive him to the rural field in suburban Kansas where he was shot to death.)

Brushing aside personal threats, Mike and Ike went on building the business. In January 1933, they leased an additional 20,000 square feet in a Kansas City warehouse, increasing their inventory and distribution space from 35,000 to 55,000 square feet. A year later the company reported the best earnings of its history, with sales for 1933 up about 10 percent from 1932.

In 1934, with eight stores, the Katz company realized a profit of $525,826 from sales of about $10 million, a company record.

Their response: Keep expanding.

That December, the chain opened the huge new, two-story "super" store at the intersection of Westport Road and Main Street in Kansas City. With 20,000 square feet, the store included a hardware department, a tire and auto service area, a balcony for toys, and a delicatessen.

It also, newspapers reported, had 29 cash registers, a $20,000 investment in itself. It was four times as large as the other Katz stores.

In missouri, unemployment was more than 38 percent.

Even the location of the store was newsworthy. It had been built in the "south" district of Kansas City, well distant of downtown, the first Katz store to be opened outside of a downtown district.

By then the Katz brothers were billing themselves as the "World's Leading Cut-Rate Druggists," and the facade of the Westport and (Continued on page 76)

RANSOMED!
THE MICHAEL KATZ KIDNAPPING

The alleged kidnappers (from second left), R.K. Cole, Albert Cruger and Eddie "Goggle-Eyed" Leonard, were arrested and charged with complicity in the Michael H. Katz abduction, but released for lack of evidence.

AT 9:30 A.M. ON MARCH, 18, 1930, Michael Katz was driving along Ward Parkway, Kansas City's grand residential boulevard, when a car came up alongside and forced him to the curb.

There was a witness, a contractor approaching in his car from a side street. He watched as a man jumped into Katz's car and raised his arm as if to strike the driver. A moment later, both cars drove off.

About five hours later, Lewis Jay Navran, a vice president of the Katz Drug company, took a call at his downtown desk.

What he heard caused him to bolt from his office and hustle several blocks to a 12th Street hotel where, in a fourth-floor room, he found his boss, Isaac Katz — Michael's older brother — slumped across a bed, devastated by the note he had just received. In Michael's handwriting, it included instructions from the kidnappers on how to proceed if the family wanted to see Michael again.

The abduction of Michael Katz was the first of three high-profile Kansas City kidnappings during the 1930s.

On Dec. 16, 1931, three abductors kidnapped wealthy dress manufacturer Nell Donnelly and her chauffeur, George Blair, at gunpoint from the driveway of her home. The kidnappers released Donnelly and Blair two days later, and two of the abductors received life sentences.

On May 27, 1933, 25-year-old Mary McElroy, daughter of City Manager Henry F. "Judge" McElroy, was kidnapped while taking a bubble bath in her father's home. She was ransomed and released physically unharmed, but committed suicide in 1940.

The abductions opened a window on the unpredictable violence of machine-era Kansas City.

The Katz kidnapping would "shatter what was left of the city's peace," wrote William M. Reddig, author of *Tom's Town*, the 1947 chronicle of machine-rule Kansas City. Michael Katz had been seized in daylight in a wealthy neighborhood, exposing the city's vulnerability to the whims of thugs.

Principal players in the drama were Michael and Isaac Katz, at least three gangsters, one of whom wore prominent glasses and had the nickname "Goggle-Eyed," and two fringe underworld individuals who served as intermediaries.

Navran, the first person Isaac Katz contacted after learning that his brother had been taken, ended up with a front-row seat on the shakedown and later wrote a memoir, which was never published and which provides some of the detail for this recounting.

By the time Navran arrived at the hotel, the kidnappers already had drafted the intermediaries. They were Bennie Portman, whom Reddig identified as a "gambler and bootlegger," and Louis "Kid" Rose, a former prizefighter. Kidnapping protocol at the time, wrote Navran, "called for the go-betweens to be members of the underworld," as they would be less eager to call the police.

By then it was late afternoon, and Navran was elected to notify Rose Katz, Michael's wife, of the kidnapping.

Eddie "Goggle-Eyed" Leonard's four-passenger coupe, shown in police impound, was wrecked by Leonard and a companion near Marshall Junction, Missouri, and left in a garage there for repairs.

"I walked into the Katz home on Ward Parkway with the disagreeable mission," Navran wrote later. "I had presence of mind enough to ask her to sit down first, fearing the words would cause her to faint. After she had been seated I did tell her about Mike's plight, and she fainted."

A second errand involved calling on Tom Pendergast, Kansas City's machine boss.

As the kidnapping had occurred near Pendergast's Ward Parkway home, the first conclusion jumped to — either by the contractor who witnessed the event or the two Kansas City police officers he hailed -- was that Tom Pendergast, Jr., the boss's son, was the victim.

That prompted its own separate drama. Pendergast summoned two northeast Kansas City criminal bosses to his 1908 Main Street office and gave them two hours to produce his son. After the men complained that they would need more time, Pendergast, then 56, attacked both of them, knocking one down and the other into a door, shattering the glass.

Ultimately, somebody confirmed that Tom Jr. was attending his usual classes at Kansas City's Rockhurst College.

The Star detailed where the kidnappers' roadster forced the Katz Packard sport coupe to the curb, and features of the house where Katz was held.

THE SCENE OF THE DRAMATIC KIDNAPING OF MILLIONAIRE DRUGGIST.

OTHER VIEWS OF A HOUSE WHERE A GANG OF EXTORTIONISTS IS BELIEVED TO HAVE CONCEALED MICHAEL KATZ.

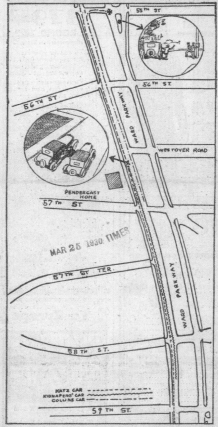

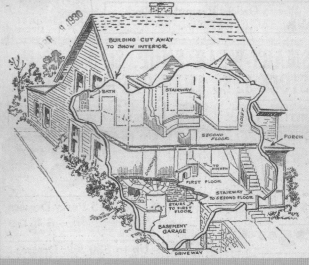

BUILDING CUT AWAY TO SHOW INTERIOR

A photographic and artist's conception of the scene along Ward parkway, near Westover road, in front of the T. J. Pendergast home, where kidnapers Tuesday afternoon overpowered "Mike" Katz, later extorting $100,000 from his brother, "Ike" Katz, for his safe return. In the photograph showing the Pendergast home in the background the cross (X) mark indicates where the kidnapers, driving a Chrysler sport roadster, forced the Katz Packard sport coupe to the curb. A man leaped from the Chrysler into the coupe. His hand was seen by Roy T. Collins, building contractor, 7241 Ward parkway, to rise and fall, as if in striking someone, and the cars moved north.

The sketch illustrates the progress of the Packard north from the Katz home at Ward parkway and Huntington road, to where the kidnapers' car intercepted it in front of the Pendergast home, just south of the intersection of Westover road, and the path of the Collins car as it trailed the other two machines, one presumably carrying the helpless druggist, to Fifty-fifth street, where Collins summoned two patrolmen standing at a call box in the parkway.

That same night, Isaac Katz and Lewis Navran called on Pendergast. "He agreed to see us," Navran wrote, "and was in a dressing gown when we arrived. He ranted and raved about the local police force, then under Republican state control. Finally, he said that if it were a local job, he could do something about it. Otherwise, his hands were completely tied."

The next morning Pendergast told Navran that it was an "out-of-town job."

Then it was back to the downtown Kansas City hotel room where the negotiating began by telephone, "opening the bidding," Reddig wrote, "for the life of Mike Katz." The kidnappers began at $200,000. Navran began at $25,000.

"The gang's agent on the telephone lost patience at one stage of the negotiations when $40,000 was offered," Reddig wrote.

" 'Say, keep your forty,' the muffled voice said. 'We'll bring him home for nothing.' "

Navran went to $50,000, then agreed to the original $100,000 demand. He walked back to the Katz offices and contacted Lewis Hoffman, another Katz executive who, in turn, contacted Commerce Trust Company. The bank provided $100,000 in cash.

Navran recorded the serial numbers of the bills and then put the money in various pockets of his suit and overcoat. He then made what likely was a highly alert walk to the 12th Street hotel.

'YOU'D BETTER COUNT IT'

"Upon reaching the Portman and Rose hotel room, I took the bills and tossed them on the bed," Navran wrote. "I told them they had better count the money. We counted and counted, and it was 20 thousand dollars short. I didn't know what to do so I ran my hands through my pockets again and I finally found a package of bills, which was the missing 20 thousand."

Portman and Rose then received more instructions. They were to drive three times around the Coates House hotel at 10th Street and Broadway, after which Portman was to go into the lobby and wait for a telephone call.

The phone rang in the lobby and Portman received still more instructions, this time to drive to a location in northeast Kansas City and leave the money wrapped in newspaper on the car seat. This they did and walked away from the car. "They heard footsteps running behind them but did not dare turn back and look," Navran wrote.

After waiting for a few moments, Portman and Rose returned to the car and drove back to the hotel, where they received one last call telling them to pick up Michael Katz at the stone colonnades at Concourse Circle, a park back in northeast Kansas City.

Navran accompanied Portman and Rose on this trip. At about 7:15 p.m. they found Katz sitting on a bench in the colonnades. According to Reddig, Katz had been instructed to keep a hood on his head for five minutes. "No one disturbed him."

Navran picks up the story: "We immediately brought him into town and delivered him to his home, safe and sound, although slightly the worse for the ordeal he had undergone." It was 36 hours since he had been snatched.

Kansas City police arrested Portman and Rose, since they were the most prominent local figures involved in the abduction. But the trail had already gone cold.

"The police were in a difficult situation," Navran said, "as they could give the newspapers no information whatever, since they actually knew nothing about it. Meanwhile the papers were making a considerable fuss about the entire situation of an unsolved crime involving a prominent businessman and a large sum of money." Ultimately Navran gave the story to Kansas City Star reporter James Jackson.

A grand jury was seated and police arrested three men, R.K. Cole, Albert Cruger and Eddie "Goggle Eyed" Leonard, but they didn't have enough evidence to hold them. While investigators determined that some of the cash had been used to buy a new Buick in Kansas City, which then was driven to St. Louis, the bulk of the $100,000 (worth perhaps $1.3 million in 2011 dollars) was never recovered.

In his account of the kidnapping, Navran suggested one possible reason why the Katz family had been targeted. It involved a naivete on Isaac's part that is difficult to imagine today.

The Katz brothers had taken their company public in 1929. According to Navran, an underwriter who assisted in the public offering gave Isaac a check for $1 million, representing 40 percent of the company stock.

Isaac made photostat facsimiles of the check and handed them out to friends and acquaintances along 12th Street. "Ike imagined that these people all took

the same pride in his accomplishment as he did," Navran wrote. "In this he was wrong, as a great many of these characters lay awake nights trying to figure out some way to get part of this million. One of them sent to St. Louis and brought in a bunch of kidnappers."

Ike and Mike increased their personal caution but still received threats. In 1933, a letter delivered to both Isaac and Michael directed that violence to the Katz family could be avoided if $60,000 were placed beneath loose planks in the floor of a North Kansas City streetcar station. Authorities planted a dummy ransom and watched from a distance. Nobody showed.

Michael, by this time, had hired a chauffeur.

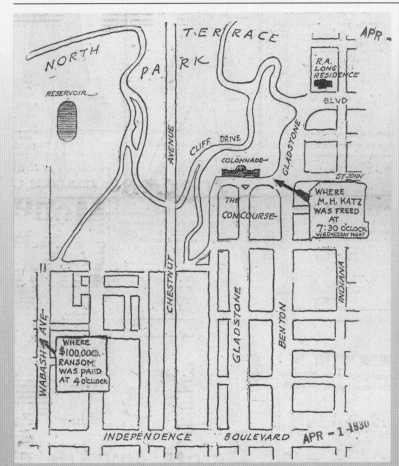

A map and photos showed the ransom drop-off spot, the colonnade where Katz was freed and the R.A. Long home.

1933

Katz tells share-
holders that
1933 is company's
best year yet,
with a net profit
of $551,538.

1934

New Katz
drugstore at
Westport Road
and Main Street
is considered
the largest in
the country.

1934

Harry Truman,
Jackson County,
Missouri presiding
judge, is elected
to U.S. Senate.

WILBORN & ASSOCIATES

An opening in Roeland Park got a typical mix of the committed and the curious.

(Continued from page 70)
Main store read "*World's Leading
Cut Rate Drug Stores.*"

Katz was keeping good company.
In 1934 a New York survey group,
Burr & Co., reported that Katz
Drug was one of five corporations
that had been able to report net
earnings higher than their
1930 levels. The others were
F.W. Woolworth, Peoples Drug,
Walgreen and S.S. Kresge.

It was during the 1930s that Katz
Drug became the store many remember today — big stores where families could get prescriptions filled, and
get almost everything else as well.

In 1935, a writer for Business
Week magazine described the "new
Katz technique of merchandizing
such 'drugs' as electric refrigerators,
radio sets, delicatessen, bicycles,
gas and oil, haberdashery…"
(Continued on page 80)

CLARENCE KIVETT

IN 1931, prominent Kansas City archiects Hoit, Price & Barnes laid off a young drafts-man, Clarence Kivovitch, a recent architecture graduate of the University of Kansas.

Kivovitch (who later worked under the name Clarence Kivett) opened his own office in the Victor Building in downtown Kansas City. One of the jobs that kept him in business was the exterior remodel of a "sundries" shop with a back room that featured "21," dice and horse-racing updates.

"These were tough times," Kivett told The Kansas City Star in 1982. "The architects were closing their offices, only I didn't know it. I didn't know from nothing. Except that I had made up my mind that before I ran totally out of money — and I had accumulated a large amount; I think I had $100 —

I was going to have my own office, at least for a month or two."

The young architect's fortunes would change with a big assignment: the new Katz "super" store at Westport Road and Main Street in Kansas City.

It was described as the world's largest drug store. The clients were Isaac and Mike Katz of the Katz Drug Company, then one of the fastest growing retail chains in the country. It would be Kivett's first try at designing a drug store.

So how did he land this commission? One reason was his mother, Anna Katz Kivett, sister to Isaac and Michael.

"Of course, it took me three years to get a job from them," the architect told The Star, "and it was only through my mother saying something to her brothers that I got it…"

The building, with its dazzling design, made a splash. One account described its principal feature as a "constructivist clock tower with boldly colored vertical

Postcard shows moderne curves of Westport store.

striping and horizontal fins." Three clocks adorned the east, north and south faces of the buff brick portion of the tower, which was topped by an aluminum flagpole.

In later years Kivett told associates how in 1933 he had visited Chicago's Century of Progress International Exposition, where he admired Paul Philippe Cret's 1933 Hall of Science carillon tower. That tower, in turn, was said to owe much to Robert Mallet-Stevens' cubist-inspired Pavillon du Tourisme at the 1925 Paris Exposition.

Other accounts of the building's design include the names "Frohwerk and Bloomgarten." The 1931 Kansas City directory lists D. Kent Frohwerk and Robert B. Bloomgarten, identifying both as draftsmen at Hoit, Price & Barnes.

In 1940 Kivett joined forces with Ralph Myers. After 1948, the firm operated for several years as Kivett & Myers & McCallum.

Today Kivett & Myers is associated with some of Kansas City's most familiar structures, from Kansas City International Airport to the twin stadiums of the Truman Sports Complex, to what is now the InterContinental Hotel on the Country Club Plaza.

In 1975 Kivett & Myers merged with Howard Needles Tammen & Bergendoff, architects, engineers and planners, and Kivett became a consultant.

Interviewers over the years continued to ask him about the Katz Drug store design. "You could say that the design was art deco, although I didn't know it at the time," Kivett told The Star. "The term became popular in the '60s."

Others were more outspoken on Kivett's behalf. According to testimony collected in 2006 by Kansas City's Landmarks Commission, his work

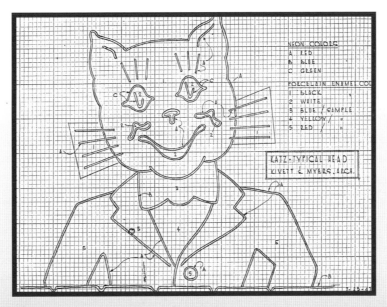

The Katz cat evolved over the years. This version for the marquee of the Kansas City Westport and Main store was rendered on graph paper at Kivett & Myers.

"stands at the forefront of the post-World War II generation of architecture in the Kansas City region.

"Clarence Kivett was a pioneering proponent of modernism in a region more inclined to traditionalism and bottom-line utilitarianism."

Today the Katz Drug store building at 3948 Main St. is considered part of the South Side Historic District — the stretch of more than 40 business and other sites along Main Street between 38th and 40th streets, built between 1920 and 1940. The district was listed on the National Register of Historic Places in 1983.

Kivett died in 1996 at the age of 91. His obituary in The Star declared him "the father of modern design in Kansas City," and noted that an elaborate diagram prepared for a party in his honor in the 1980s showed that Kivett & Myers had spawned more than 50 architectural firms.

After the sale of the Katz Company to Skaggs Corp. in 1971, the building operated under Skaggs and then the Osco names. The store closed after CVS Corp. bought Osco in 2006.

It was scheduled to be sold at auction in the summer of 2011.

1937

Katz Drug Co. underwrites the first of many Kansas City Philharmonic concerts for employees, family and friends.

1937

Two-week strike by Katz Drug employees closes some stores.

1937

Sale of 3.2 percent beer is approved in Kansas, the first relaxing of state liquor laws since 1880.

In 1933, Shetland ponies were sold at Katz auctions in Kansas City, St. Joseph and Des Moines.

(Continued from page 76)

A TOUCH OF HOLLYWOOD

The brothers had a touch for show business.

They organized "Million Dollar Sales" at which customers received coupons, or "Katz cash," that they then could use to bid on items at a Katz auction in a downtown convention hall.

In December 1933, in Kansas City's Convention Hall, a Kansas City boy bought a Shetland pony with $52,050 in paper "bucks." A second Shetland pony was auctioned off that year in St. Joseph, and a third in Des Moines.

There were the inevitable problems. A Kansas City police captain had to respond to a complaint filed by Nellie Dezulski of Independence Avenue. Dezulski, who apparently raised poultry at her home, had sold a goose to a customer for $2. The customer got the goose and $8 in change after Nellie accepted what she discovered,
(Continued on page 84)

DEPRESSION OR NO DEPRESSION

---You Saved Nearly Two Million Dollars at Katz Last Year!

A NEW YEAR'S MESSAGE FROM THE Katz DRUG CO.

IT takes more than a business depression to lick Katz. The past year has demonstrated that. Backed by its hundreds of thousands of loyal patrons, Katz marched on to a new sales record in 1931, and at the same time saved the public the tremendous sum of $1,792,000!

No depression can lick Katz because no depression can lick the people. Katz represents the people. Not the rich, not the wealthy and affluent, but the hard-working, job-holding people who come to Katz in ever increasing numbers because Katz's low prices make their hard-earned dollars go farther.

To these people the Katz stores owe their existence, and to them Katz acknowledges a lasting obligation to serve which is binding on every member of the Katz organization, from the lowest to the highest.

In reviewing the past year, Katz feels both proud and humble. Proud because of growth and increased sales. Humble because these increases are mainly attributable to the need of the people for buying more carefully, more keenly, more SAVINGLY than ever before.

Whatever the new year holds in store for Katz, Katz will keep faith with its customers. We pledge that at our stores you will always be able to buy standard, nationally known merchandise at the greatest savings possible for us to provide.

To Kansas City, to you and yours—Happy New Year!

THE KATZ DRUG COMPANY
By
m. k katz
PRESIDENT

Here Is An Example of How Katz Saves You Money

	Regular Price	Katz Price
Lambert's Listerine	$1.00	59c
Bayer's Aspirin	1.25	72c
Ingram's Shaving Cream	.50	28c
Caldwell's Syrup of Pepsin	1.20	68c
Lucky Tiger Hair Tonic	1.00	59c
Hind's Honey & Almond Cream	.50	28c
Pebeco Tooth Paste	.50	28c
Palmolive Shaving Cream	.35	19c
Kotex	.45	19c
Gillette Razor Blades	1.00	57c
Grove's Bromo Quinine	.30	18c
Sal Hepatica	1.20	68c
Mentholatum	.60	36c
	$9.85	$5.59

Total Cost at Regular Prices	$9.85
Total Cost at Katz's Prices	$5.59
The Difference	$4.26

You Save $4.26—Nearly Half!

You can thank Katz for deep-cut drug prices in Kansas City. Katz has led the way since 1916. Katz has made it possible for you to buy standard, nationally advertised merchandise at an average saving of 20% over established prices. The millions of dollars Katz has saved the people of Kansas City has been a real factor in raising the living standard of this community above that of other American cities.

Katz maintains its sensational low prices by large scale buying, rapid turnover and scientific store management. Rapid turnover likewise insures the quality of all Katz merchandise. Drugs never gather dust and lose strength on Katz shelves.

Buy regularly at Katz. The $4.26 saving on the $9.85 bill of goods, as illustrated above, is typical of the substantial savings you can enjoy.

Remember—more than 25,000 items are on sale at deep-cut prices every day in the year at Katz stores!

IT'S AN OLD Katz CUSTOM

Each year an increase in sales ... in 1931 the greatest increase of all.

OUR 1ST YEAR IN BUSINESS **$12,171**

RETAIL VOLUME FOR 1931 **$7,749,206**

We realize that public confidence in the Katz Drug Company must be based upon certain fundamental principles: the unfailing quality of our merchandise; a gratifying sales volume that shows strong demand for those products; faith in the soundness of our company and its policies; and the good will of the industry of which we are a part.

1916 — Katz Pays the Tax — 1932

HAPPY NEW YEAR · HAPPY NEW YEAR
COPYRIGHT 1921 BY ILM KATZ

Customers at the Million Dollar Sales got money-saving coupons — and coins and scrip known as "Katz cash," which drew thousands to auctions at convention halls in Kansas City and other cities.

Multitudes of drug store customers eager to spend "Katz cash"
at auction packed Kansas City's Convention Hall Nov. 5, 1936.
A successful bid wouldn't cost the buyer a penny.

KATZ DRUG Co - AUCTION
NOV 5. 1936.

(Continued from page 80)
the next morning, was $10 of "Katz cash."

Mike and Ike leveraged the city's robust love of sports. Once a year during the '30s, Katz stores distributed free tickets to a game of the minor league Kansas City Blues baseball team.

In August, 1933, each customer who bought a tube of Dr. West's tooth paste at Katz received a ticket to see the Blues play the Columbus Red Birds. More than 16,000 baseball fans received free tickets.

The next summer, a similar Katz promotion attracted an estimated 36,200 baseball fans to Kansas City's Muehlebach Field at 22nd and Brooklyn, the largest crowd ever seen for a Kansas City baseball game. The crowd overwhelmed the

facility, with many fans ending up on the field, crowding the foul lines and parting only for the occasional foul ball.

A KATZ PROMOTION ATTRACTED 36,200 BASEBALL FANS TO MUEHLEBACH FIELD, OVERWHELMING THE PARK.

Katz was on the radio, sponsoring the weekend Nighthawk Jamborees at the Uptown Theater in Kansas City over WDAF.

For a brief time, Katz stores also featured slot machines. Gambling

It was August of '33, and customers who bought a tube of Dr. West's at a Katz store got a free ticket to the ball game.

Not long after the turn of the century, Isaac and his youngest brother,
Michael, began a business partnership that would last a lifetime.
In this 1944 photo, Isaac (left) would have been about 65, Michael 56.

A humidor was just a humidor unless it was embossed with the Katz Drugs name and logo.

was widely available in 1930s Kansas City, with slot machines in many stores and restaurants.

But in August 1933, the machine politicians who regulated the city's gambling pulled back on the industry, and the slot machines were removed from many restaurants and stores, including the Katz brothers'. That also was the year Katz decided to fight the price-fixing provisions of the National Industrial Recovery Act.

THE COMPANY AGREED TO ITS FIRST UNION CONTRACT AFTER A 10-DAY STRIKE.

That 1933 legislation, signed by Franklin Roosevelt, was designed to level the playing field for strapped retailers during the Depression. It regulated the number of hours employees could work in a week and set minimum prices retailers could charge for merchandise. It prohibited some discounts on tobacco products, and even stopped stores from giving away more than one pad of free matches with each cigar sold.

In July 1933, Katz was among the companies that immediately signed the NIRA agreements distributed to retailers by Federal agents. Michael Katz even sent a telegram, stating that the company would hire extra employees in order to bring all of its stores into line with the act's employment provisions.

PRICE WARS

But by that September the Katz chain had joined with the Mail Order Association of America in protesting provisions in the NIRA that fixed consumer prices at 10 percent above the highest wholesale price in a market area.

Under those rules, huge retail

giants like Sears and Montgomery Ward — and Katz — would not be able to leverage their purchasing power to negotiate lower wholesale prices which they could then pass on to their customers.

Why, the execs wondered, should big suppliers have to live with prices set by the smallest outfits? Katz joined Sears and Montgomery Ward in the protest.

In papers filed in Washington, the Katz brothers noted that the government believed "price-fixing provisions are necessary to prevent so called 'predatory price-cutting.'" But no one, the

When Katz prevailed in court, securing the right to sell the Flexible Shaft mixer at a discount price, they took out ads sharing the news.

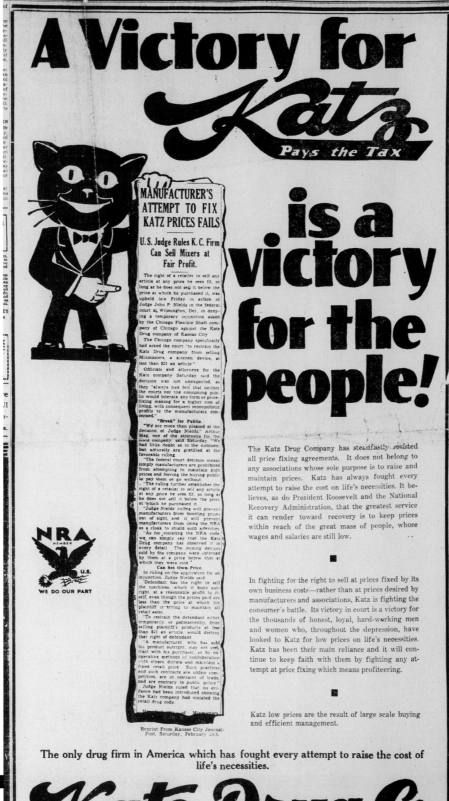

document argued, "has ever defined just what this term means."

And when it came time to challenge the retailers on this front, it wasn't Sears or Montgomery Ward that was targeted — it was Katz.

In a 1934 federal court action watched across the nation, the Chicago Flexible Shaft Company, which manufactured a household mixer, sued Katz. They accused the Katz chain of selling its Mixmaster below the $21 manufacturer's suggested retail price.

Mike and Ike, through their attorney Arthur Mag, insisted that Flexible Shaft was trying to use the NIRA to "fix" retail prices and force the public "to pay exorbitant prices with consequent monopolistic profits."

Katz stores, Mag said, sold "standard merchandise at the lowest possible prices. It does not sell below cost. It sold Mixmasters at a profit."

Isaac Katz, with Mag, traveled to Wilmington, Delaware, to wit-ness arguments in federal court.

In late February, the federal judge sided with Katz, refusing to issue the injunction sought by Flexible Shaft. The judge ruled that Katz had the right to sell the mixers at a reasonable profit even though the prices were less than those sought by the manufacturer. For the manufacturer to attempt to dictate prices, the judge said, would represent a restraint of trade.

THE KATZ BROTHERS BENEFITED FROM THE WIDESPREAD PRACTICE OF DOCTORS PRESCRIBING ALCOHOL TO PATIENTS FOR "MEDICINAL" PURPOSES.

Stories reporting the judge's decision appeared in papers across the country, including the New York Herald-Tribune, and comment came from many corners.

Business Week believed the NIRA's price fixing provisions had been aimed specifically at Katz. The Kansas City Times, the morning edition of The Star, said the decision meant the public would not be denied the opportunity to benefit from savings that a retailer had made possible "through sales in large quantities and by efficient management."

The Katz brothers were in federal court twice in 1934. The other time they asked Kansas City judge Albert Reeves for a restraining order against the part of the Federal regulations that prohibited discounts such as four "nickel cigars" for 15 cents.

It was the Depression, and cigar-smokers who could afford it needed a cigar.

Katz sold cigars for a nickel. So did other retailers around Kansas City. Since the collapse of

the stock maket, tobacco dealers had brought back the five-cent cigar for the duration of the financial emergency.

But Katz also sold four nickel cigars for 15 cents. And that was against the express wishes of the Federal guidelines.

Judge Reeves found sufficient cause to issue a temporary injunction against enforcement of the NIRA price-fixing provisions on tobacco. Federal courts in Kansas and Iowa, where Katz also had stores, issued similar injunctions.

That meant that, until the U.S. Supreme Court ruled the National Industrial Recovery Act unconstitutional the following May, the law prohibiting such tobacco discounts was never enforced in Kansas City.

Some drug stores could claim low prices; the Katz brothers went to federal court to keep them low.

In 1935, they opened their 10th store in Sioux City, Iowa.

Katz razor blades ("made of Swedish steel") were probably one thing the company had in mind when it claimed to be "The only drug firm in America which has fought every attempt to raise the cost of life's necessities."

Smokers of the day could buy a carton of 200 Lucky Strikes, Camels, Old Gold or Chesterfields for $1.19 with a Katz coupon clipped from the newspaper. Cigars were bargains, too.

They opened store number 11 in Oklahoma City in 1936. They put stores 12 and 13 into St. Louis.

By January 1938, Katz Drug Company would be operating 13 stores and employing more than 1,000.

They had to make some concessions. In July 1937, the company agreed to its first union contract after a 10-day strike in Kansas City by about 700 employees.

Their penny-shaving policies continued to rankle competitors.

In 1962 Tom Evans, a friend of Harry Truman and an executive in the Crown Drug chain, recalled the tobacco wars with Katz Drug. "We had a competitor there in Kansas City," Evans said in a Truman Library oral history. "I'm sure you've heard of them, Katz Drug Company — who, I think, gave me these gray hairs that I have — who would sell merchandise at cost and below cost…"

A pack of cigarettes actually cost about 11 and a fraction cents, Evans said, and Crown sold them for 13 cents, or two packs for a quarter.

"And we got into a price war with Katz and they advertised them at two packs for 23 and I came out at two for 22.

KATZ SOLD CIGARS FOR A NICKEL, AND FOUR NICKEL CIGARS FOR 15 CENTS.

"Then they came out at two for 21, and I came out at two for 19.

"And we were finally down selling cigarettes at five cents a package and paying 11 and a fraction."

As so often seemed to happen, the winners in that price war were the cigarette smokers and the Katz brothers.

Announcing...
THE NEW VACCUM PACKED TIN OF

NEW VACUUM PACKED

BLENDED WITH HAVANA

HEADLINE CIGARS

KEEPS HEADLINE CIGARS, FAMOUS FLAVOR AND AROMA FACTORY FRESH

FOR YOUR SMOKING PLEASURE

25 CIGARS $1.39

LOW PRICE $1.39 25 CIGARS

About This Photo

Smoking was a harmless pastime, and a well-stocked counter was part of the pleasure.

BENEFITING THE JEWISH COMMUNITY

Menorah Hospital, shown in a 1930 photograph, benefited from Katz family gifts.

"Ike loves such coincidences in this constant drama of living," wrote Kansas City Star reporter Richard B. Fowler in a 1949 story. But the anecdote also illustrates the vast satisfaction that acts of charity, both small and large, brought Isaac and his brother.

"Oh, I do love to enjoy my money," Isaac told Fowler.

Both brothers were generous benefactors to the city but especially the Jewish community, which in the 1930s numbered about 30,000 residents.

Isaac Katz was a principal organizer in 1933 when the Jewish Welfare Federation in Kansas City planned its first annual drive to fund more than 30 Jewish relief and charitable agencies. That year he donated a sum that reportedly resolved most of a $60,000 deficit at Keneseth Israel-Beth Sholom synagogue at 3400 the Paseo.

That September he made the first of many donations of state-of-the-art medical equipment to Jewish Memorial Hospital (later named Menorah) with the donation of an "artificial pacemaker,

ONCE ON A TRIP TO PALESTINE Isaac and Minnie Katz received several gift baskets as their ocean liner prepared to depart. Isaac took the largest basket of flowers and asked a steward to identify which passenger might appreciate it.

"That old woman at the rail," the steward told him. "They call her the Angel of Minneapolis and she is going to Palestine to die." Isaac presented the flowers to the woman and asked her name, which was Kieferstein. It rang a bell.

Did she have a son named Charley? She did. Then Isaac told her that it had been her son, Charley Kieferstein, who told him, after he lost his job in St. Paul, to try Kansas City.

described in The Star as a "recently invented electro-chemical device for the restoration of life to a person dead from shock to the heart."

In December Isaac endowed four beds at the hospital for the exclusive use of charity patents.

"In recent years an increasing share of communal responsibility has been taken by the Katz family," the Kansas City Jewish Chronicle reported in May 1934, "and in our just concluded Jewish Welfare Federation Campaign, no family has played quite so illustrious a role as has the House of Katz!"

One theory holds that Isaac and Michael Katz felt a more profound need to support charities in Kansas City after Michael's kidnapping in 1930. That may be partly true, although many acts of generosity preceded that trauma.

The brothers' philanthropy continued well after their deaths, Isaac's in 1956 and Michael's in 1962. A new outdoor swimming pool opened in 1957 at the new Jewish Community Center, 8201 Holmes Road in Kansas City. It was named for Michael Katz. In 1965 Katz family members helped dedicate the Isaac and Michael Katz Memorial Pharmacy Building on the campus of the University of Missouri-Kansas City.

UMKC's Katz Hall housed the pharmacy school.

But perhaps Isaac's greatest physical legacy in Kansas City was the Keneseth Israel-Beth Sholom synagogue.

The synagogue's roots dated to 1878, when Russian and Polish immigrants formed their own burial society. Keneseth Israel-Beth Sholom synagogue organized in 1924 when two separate religious communities — Keneseth Israel and Beth Sholom — merged to complete a structure on land purchased at 34th Street and the Paseo.

Isaac, Fowler added, was one of the main signers on a $125,000 note to complete construction. The finished facility was dedicated in 1927 and by the early 1930s, Isaac Katz had become one of its most important members.

But there was another reason for Isaac's sponsorship. His parents, Frank and Sarah, were members of the congregation. While the synagogue was being developed, they left St. Paul and moved into Ike and Minnie's Mission Hills mansion.

But, Fowler wrote, the elder Katzes didn't feel at home amid the Oriental rugs, custom-installed pipe organ and constant stream of visitors. They instead chose to move to midtown Kansas City, within walking distance of the synagogue.

Although its congregation moved south to a new building at Bannister and Wornall roads in the early 1960s, the synagogue that Isaac Katz helped build still stands, and is now a pentecostal church.

Frank and Sarah Katz attended Keneseth Israel-Beth Sholom synagogue at 39th and Paseo.

SUPER STORES

THE FAT YEARS

There are faint clouds on the horizon, but Katz has captured the public imagination — and pocketbook — by giving customers more than a drugstore should be able to provide.

A CROWD OF 3,000 had gathered in the street by 6 a.m.

By 7 a.m., the throng's leading edge was pushing against the glass doors at a store at the corner of Troost Avenue and Linwood Boulevard in Kansas City, Missouri. It was July 1946.

The next month, police were dispatched to maintain order in a similar crowd at the corner of Eighth Street and Washington Avenue in St. Louis.

In September 1948, something similar happened in the 700 block of Minnesota Avenue in Kansas City, Kansas. This time a store manager barely controlled the crowd, allowing only a handful through the doors every few minutes in a vain effort to observe the fire code.

The stores hadn't just put Eddie Fisher or Frank Sinatra concert tickets on sale, or had access to some other teen idol — although the company involved would later have a brush with the biggest teen idol of them all.

The excitement was generated by the opening of a Katz Drug store in the neighborhood. Between 1940 and 1956, the company stretched the concept of "drug store" beyond anything previously imagined. With dazzling success.

The top draw probably was the sheer array of goods. Throughout the 1940s, Katz executives claimed to stock more than 35,000 individual items in each location. That included sporting goods, cameras and cosmetics, rubber playground balls made in Japan

1941

Katz introduces "self-service" concept; customers pass through a turnstile to enter the store and carry items to the checkout counter.

1942

Third store opens in St. Louis, 19th store in Katz chain.

1948

Katz reduces inventory of grocery items in stores after tension between Katz and grocery store operators.

Katz began selling grocery items: coffee, canned nuts, cereal, crackers and flour, which was unwelcome competition for neighboring grocers.

(after the 1941 Japanese attack on Pearl Harbor, donated to a local rubber drive), clocks, shirts, hosiery and many varieties of alcohol.

By the late 1940s, the inventory grew more dizzying, including live animals such as monkeys, alligators and piranha fish. By 1954, the company claimed to be the country's second largest retailer of exotic birds, with more than 35,000 sold the previous year.

The stores began to carry grocery items, a sore point with grocery chains operating in the same territories as Katz.

Everything inside the doors was offered at low prices, too low for competing merchants. One regional trade publication called the Katz company "ruthless." Lawmakers in Missouri and Oklahoma drafted "fair trade" bills that, they said, would establish minimum retail prices.

In 1948, three African-Americans were refused service at the lunch counter of the Des Moines Katz store. Such refusals were common practice, in no way exclusive to Katz. What was unusual is that the store manager was convicted of violating the state's civil rights laws. It was a foretaste of the coming struggle for equal access to public accommodations.

BY 1954, KATZ WOULD CLAIM AN AVERAGE OF 225,000 CUSTOMERS A DAY.

But the conviction didn't seem to penetrate the ranks of Katz executives. Ten years later, another lunch counter incident in Oklahoma would become a civil rights landmark case.

But there was no doubt about the grip that Katz Drugs had on *(Continued on page 99)*

African-American customers wait to be served at the Katz Drug store lunch counter in Oklahoma City, August 26, 1958. Days earlier, history teacher Clara Luper had begun the sit-in, which succeeded in integrating Katz counters.

A powerful searchlight announces the grand opening of the Roeland Park, Kansas, store in 1951. It's probably safe to say that the ferris wheel was part of the celebration.

(Continued from page 96)

the imaginations of shoppers in Des Moines, St. Louis, Kansas City, Oklahoma City, Sioux City and — as of 1954 — Memphis, the home town of that teen idol.

The St. Louis opening "drew a greater crowd than had ever stormed the doors at the opening of a new drug outlet."
— from the trade publication Tobacco Leaf

By August 1954, the chain would claim an average of 255,000 customers a day, served by more than 3,000 employees.

The company maintained a high cultural profile in Kansas City, its headquarters, sponsoring annual free Philharmonic orchestra concerts beginning in 1944. The brothers booked headliners such as opera star Rise Stevens, pianist Oscar Levant, and clarinetist and band leader Benny Goodman.

It was while on his way to one Philharmonic concert in 1954 that teen phenom Eddie Fisher was knocked to the sidewalk by a group of teenage girls who ambushed him outside the doors of his downtown Kansas City hotel.

That same year Elvis Presley performed at the opening of the Memphis store. Not only was decorum maintained, the unknown performer wasn't even mentioned in the local newspaper coverage of the opening.

But any Katz opening resembled a kind of civic emergency.

They combined elements of homecoming parades (marching bands, as at the Kansas City, Kansas opening) movie premieres (searchlights combing the sky), you-are-there immediacy (live radio station remote broadcasts), and sometimes the police.

The same process was repeated almost every time. Newspaper readers would encounter several pages of advertising days before the (Continued on page 103)

PARKING LOT ROCK

ON SEPT. 9, 1954, the manager of the new Katz Drugs store in Memphis, Tennessee, budgeted $20 for opening night entertainment.

He set aside $10 for a flatbed truck. The truck, parked in the back parking lot, would serve as a stage for the band.

The other $10 was for the band: three Memphis musicians who had released their first record only weeks before. One of those musicians was Elvis Presley, and the Katz parking lot concert was one of his first paying engagements.

So says Colleen Roberts of Edgerton, Missouri, who would know. Her father, Peter Morton, was the Katz Drug store manager who hired Elvis.

Few retail chains can claim to have played a pivotal role in the early career of the King. Katz can.

For those who keep and maintain the Elvis Day-By-Day Narrative, the September 9, 1954, show at the new Memphis Katz Drugs was probably the one that convinced Presley and his two band mates, guitarist Scotty Moore and bassist Bill Black, that they were onto something. They were just two months removed from recording Presley's first songs at Sun Studio in Memphis.

Two of those songs — "That's All Right" and "Blue Moon of Kentucky" — had been Elvis' first 45 rpm record release, and those two songs had been playing long enough on Memphis radio stations to attract a large crowd to the new Lamar-Airways Shopping Center, for which the new Katz Drugs served as anchor.

> "IT WAS THE KIDS' RESPONSE THAT DROVE THE MUSIC TO ANOTHER LEVEL. IT WAS SO OUT OF CONTROL IT WAS ALMOST FRIGHTENING."
> — PETER GURALNICK, ELVIS BIOGRAPHER, ON KATZ OPENING NIGHT

The show was scheduled to begin at 9 p.m.

What happened then would be described and remembered in various ways.

Peter Guralnick, in *Last Train to Memphis: The Rise of Elvis Presley*, said the crowd assembled in the parking lot was "made up almost exclusively of teenagers."

Among them was Opal Walker, who took several photographs of Elvis.

"I rode a streetcar, I believe, and waited for Elvis to arrive," Walker said.

"They all came up in that Chevy and I asked him to pose and he seemed happy to. There were a lot of people there, but few besides me seemed to know who he was. I had him all to myself. I could have shot a whole roll.

"He went on stage and started singing and shaking…the girls went wild. Me, too."

Another person in the crowd was a recently-released airman from the U.S. Air Force, Johnny Cash, just starting his own career.

"The first time I saw Elvis, singing from a flatbed truck at a Katz drugstore opening on Lamar Avenue, two or three hundred people, mostly teenaged girls, had come out to see him," Cash wrote in his 1997 autobiography.

"With just one single to his credit, he sang those two songs over and over."

The teenagers didn't care.

It was, Guralnick wrote, "the kids' response that drove the music to another level. It was so out of control it was almost frightening."

Guralnick also quoted Scotty Moore as saying that the response made an impact on the three musicians.

"This was the first time we could see what was happening," Moore said. " 'Cause it was a whole parking lot full of kids, and they just went crazy."

The world knows the rest of the story. But what still interests Colleen Roberts was how Elvis kept coming back to Katz Drugs.

"Elvis and my Dad would become very good friends," she said. Several times Elvis asked Morton for permission to come by the store after closing time.

"He could have had anything he wanted by then, but he liked to shop at Katz," Roberts said. "He was very down to earth, and didn't put on any airs."

The day-by-day Elvis chronicles do record one apparently extravagant Katz Drugs purchase: a monkey, bought on October 25, 1960.

Price: $123.55

But Elvis's performance fees had increased by then.

COURTESY OPAL WALKER

Still relatively unknown, Elvis Presley, guitar player Scotty Moore (left) and bassist Bill Black played the Katz Drugs parking lot in the Lamar-Airways Shopping Center in Memphis, Sept. 9, 1954.

The opening of a Katz Drug store in a new city almost always caused a disturbance in civic life. As this page in the St. Louis Daily Globe-Democrat illustrates, it was preceded by many pages of newspaper ads that spelled out in alluring detail what benefits and sights awaited the new Katz customer.

(Continued from page 99)
opening. The August 1946 opening of the 8th and Washington store in St. Louis was preceded by five pages of advertising in the Post-Dispatch.

That opening, wrote the St. Louis correspondent for the trade publication Tobacco Leaf, "drew a greater crowd than had ever stormed the doors at the opening of a new drug outlet." As the cigar department manager added, Tobacco Leaf reported "record sales." Also, the police were called in for crowd control.

Often the newspaper advertisements promised free gifts to customers. Those who reported to the Kansas City, Kansas, opening in 1948 were given 8,000 balloons,

7,000 beanies and several thousand orchids. In a nod to highbrows, the opening the same year of the Katz location in North Kansas City featured *Tobacco Road* author Erskine Caldwell signing copies of his books.

The result at most openings was a frenzy of shoppers barely kept at bay until the official ribbon had been cut, usually by an oversized pair of scissors wielded by Isaac or Michael Katz — or in later years, by Isaac's son Earl. In 1946, when the customers waiting outside the newly expanded Linwood and Troost store were allowed in, they purchased 100 electric fans in the first 14 minutes.

It was, after all, July.

Once the doors were opened at the newly expanded Linwood and Troost store, customers bought 100 electric fans in 14 minutes — the price of the fans is lost to history.

WILBORN & ASSOCIATES

Katz executives, including Morris Shlensky (second left), Earl Katz (right) and an unnamed Miss Independence, officiated at the grand opening of an Independence, Missouri, store Jan. 31, 1967.

THE NEIGHBORHOOD STORE BECOMES A 'DESTINATION'

The steady march of store openings and reopenings continued through the 1940s. At the beginning of the decade, the Katz chain did report a slight dip in sales.

Company officials responded with an aggressive expansion campaign, with new or renovated stores opening in quick succession. In June 1941 executives announced a new store in Oklahoma City, the 19th Katz store. The 20th store, the company announced that year, would stand at 75th Street and Broadway, in the Waldo district of then south Kansas City.

Both the daily and trade press considered these openings newsworthy, and sometimes were compelled to describe what the Katz Drug shopping experience included.

"Merchandise and more merchandise," one publication reported in May 1941. "That fact stands out in the customers' minds as they walk down the aisles of the store. There is no attempt to display it prettily; instead, it is heaped as high as possible, and below the tables there are cartons of still more merchandise. *(Continued on page 110)*

Time magazine, Sports Illustrated, pipes, and neat rows of cigars in open boxes welcomed men to a Katz tobacco counter in 1955.

KATZ ADVERTISING PHILOSOPHY: DO IT

THE KATZ DRUG COMPANY advertised in newspapers like a sailor on leave enjoyed alcoholic beverages. So said the Independent Merchant, a St. Louis-area retail trade publication in 1936.

The actual remark, "Katz is spending money for advertising like a drunken sailor," was prompted by several pages of advertising the company placed in the St. Louis Post-Dispatch after the November opening of its first store in that city.

The statement was not made in any light-hearted way, as a long list of St. Louis merchants saw the entry of Katz Drugs into their trade area as a real threat.

While plenty of merchants in other cities harbored similar feelings, the St. Louis episode would escalate, with several Katz employees actually being arrested in December for allegedly violating the state's Sunday sales law. The law dated to the 1820s, banned the sale of non-essential merchandise, and had not been vigorously enforced for years. But that was before Katz Drugs arrived in town.

Over its approximately 55-year history, Katz would advertise relentlessly, especially in newspapers. It bought radio time beginning in the early 1940s, after the company aired 1,540 spots over 10 weeks in the final quarter of 1941. At the same time it contracted with United Film Ad, the Kansas City company that hired young artist Walt Disney after World War I, to film one-minute commercials that played in Kansas City theaters located close to Katz stores.

It found increasingly novel ways to get its name and signature cat in front of customers.

Kansas City radio listeners in 1934 could check the correct time on the "Katz Musical Clock," a daily morning show broadcast over WDAF which included, along with popular dance tunes played by a studio orchestra, the correct time every five minutes.

The company sponsored radio broadcasts of Big Six college football for sports fans and, once a year, distributed tickets to a game of the minor-league Kansas City Blues.

The company's annual "moneyless" auctions, which sometimes included

KATZ PARKED A 40-TON PRESERVED WHALE OUTSIDE THE WESTPORT AND MAIN STORE.

name entertainment, sometimes were broadcast over WDAF, as was the Katz Uptown Nighthawk Jamboree, an amateur talent contest conducted during the 1930s.

When the Sioux City, Iowa, Katz store prepared for its annual Million Dollar Sale in 1935, the company affixed a billboard to a specially chartered streetcar and ran it back and forth over city streetcar tracks. In December 1953, Katz parked a 40-ton preserved whale outside the Westport and Main store, one day drawing 3,800 curious residents,

To kick off its annual Million Dollar Sale Katz had a two-night party for employees, a dress-up event.

some of whom also may have gone inside the store.

But the company spent the most money on its full-page or center-spread newspaper advertisements. In several pages of ads in The Kansas City Star in November 1931, Katz highlighted these bargains in advance of its Million Dollar Sale:

- a two-quart hot water bottle: 39 cents
- a pack of Bicycle playing cards: 34 cents
- 5-cent cigars, seven for 25 cents
- window shades: three for 25 cents
- 18 karat solid-gold wedding bands: $3.95
- genuine diamond rings with 18 karat solid gold band: $6.95

Among the drug-related items:
- 50-cent Pepsodent toothpaste: 28 cents
- 35-cent package of laxative pills: 24 cents

Such advertising proved too much for some in St. Louis. On Dec. 5, 1936, Katz Drug ran an eight-page, color Post-Dispatch advertisement that was called the biggest drug ad ever placed in a St. Louis paper. It wasn't the size as much as the prices listed that alarmed competing merchants.
- Vicks Vapo-Rub, normally 35 cents: 26 cents
- A 25-cent bottle of Bayer aspirin: 12 cents

The executives of rival drug stores were forced to respond. "Sure! Low prices but no ballyhoo at Parks!" read one such ad.

Mere days after the December 5 advertisement, St. Louis police arrested the manager and an employee of the Katz store at 7th and Locust streets for selling a $7 radio on Sunday in violation of a state law that made the sale of merchandise considered non-essential a misdemeanor. Police officers returned the following two Sundays and made similar arrests. On the third Sunday of December, the same Katz store manager was arrested twice while police made separate morning and afternoon visits, witnessing the sale of an alarm clock and an electric toaster in the morning and the sale of a tie clasp in the afternoon.

Some newspaper editors — who greatly admired the Katz Drug company, given their fondness for advertising in their pages -- were puzzled. The St. Louis Globe Democrat wondered why the 19th century law was being "revived."

Three days before Christmas, a St. Louis prosecuting attorney explained. Those retailers who had been arrested, he said, were "chiselers who hide behind some

screen to sell seven days a week in competition with other merchants who are satisfied to do business six days a week."

Complaints, the prosecutor added, had been received from the Retail Druggists Association, the Retail Furniture Dealers Association and Independence Inc. That was the trade group representing independent merchants and whose publication had referred to Katz as a drunken sailor.

Katz Drug indeed was dinged by the St. Louis Better Business Bureau for some practices that fall, such as advertising a "$15.95" auto heater "on sale" for $8.95, which was its actual list price, and some discrepancies between prices asked inside the store and those advertised in the store window. The arrests continued into January, and ultimately 11 Katz employees were charged with conspirac to violate the state Sunday laws. The resolution of these charges can't be located in the newspaper clippings file maintained over the years by Katz secretaries.

But Katz was in St. Louis to stay.

In February 1937, the company announced the pending opening of its second store in Wellston, just northwest o the city limits.

1950s

1954

Katz company observes 40th birthday.

1954

Elvis Presley celebrates the opening of a Memphis shopping center with truck bed concert in parking lot outside new Katz store.

1955

Kansas City goes major league, Kansas City Athletics play their first game.

1956

Isaac Katz dies Nov. 9, age 77.

WILBORN & ASSOCIATES

In this 1955 store interior shot, a savvy manager has put records up front (45's left, albums right), where they'll catch the eyes of teens and 20 somethings.

(Continued from page 104)
Other writers, however, discerned true production values. "Its brilliant florescent lighting and gleaming fixtures make it one of the most modern and attractive stores in St. Louis," reported the Wellston Journal in January 1942, describing a new store in a district just northwest of the St. Louis city limits.

It featured all the regular Katz departments, including electrical, cutlery, sporting goods, toilet goods, feminine hygiene, jewelry, toys, tobacco and liquor. There also was a "Health House" department, with a medical consultant dispensing advice.

The St. Louis Post-Dispatch, describing the 8th and Washington store in 1946, noted how the large, square supporting posts had been outfitted with mirrors at about the counter level, "eliminating a feeling that they obstructed a general view of the store." Wide aisles had been designed to carry a maximum number of shoppers, directed between "blond finished wood counters."

Another trade publication article that year described in considerable detail the engineering behind the prescriptions counter in the newly-renovated store at Linwood and Troost in Kansas City.

It had a stainless steel counter, as well as a work bench 6 feet long, 40 inches high and 24 inches wide. A total of 165 drawers held tablets, capsules, ointments and ampules.
(Continued on page 115)

ICE COLD BEE
SERVE YOURSELF

TONICS & VITAMINS

PATENT MEDICINES

PKG of 6
19¢

Candy Bars
2 for 5

IN 1954, ISAAC AND MICHAEL KATZ invited former President Harry Truman to help celebrate the 40th anniversary of the Katz Drug Company.

Notes at the Truman Library in Independence indicate that the former president, though recovering from gall bladder surgery, agreed to meet the Katz brothers "for cake" at his downtown Kansas City office. (It was before the presidential library opened in Independence.)

Truman likely received many invitations. Perhaps he remembered Isaac Katz for the $200 he'd donated to the 1934 "Truman for Senate" campaign. A former Jackson County presiding judge, Truman had been personally selected to run for the seat by Kansas City Democratic machine boss Tom Pendergast. For that donation, Katz received a thank you note from Roger T. Sermon, a Truman campaign official and future Independence mayor.

The same year, the donor rolls recorded a $250 gift from Isaac Katz to the local

THE FORMER PRESIDENT "ADMITTED THAT HE WISHED HE HAD OPENED A DRUG STORE INSTEAD OF A HABERDASHERY..."

Democratic Party's municipal election campaign, which would have supported those candidates placed on the ballot by the same Pendergast organization.

In making that donation Isaac Katz was in powerful company. The list of donors included H. F. McElroy, the Pendergast-affiliated city manager; Bryce Smith, Kansas City's mayor; Nell Quinland Reed, owner of the Donnelly Garment Company, which manufactured the "Nelly Don" line of women's apparel; and T.L. Evans.

That quite likely was Tom L. Evans, one of Truman's closest political associates and himself a longtime Kansas City area drug store owner and executive with Crown Drug, a Katz competitor.

But the files at the Truman Library include only minor correspondence between Truman and the Katz family.

In May 1945, a few weeks after Franklin Roosevelt died and Truman became president, Marvin Katz, son of Michael, wrote to Truman asking permission for himself and his father to come by the White House and extend greetings.

The president agreed, and on June 4, 1945, Michael and Marvin Katz got 15 minutes with Truman at the White House

According to the day's calendar, this followed the 15-minute visit of Arthur Bliss Lane, U.S. ambassador to Poland.

Truman was well regarded in the Kansas City area Jewish community, not only for his work after World War II on behalf of Europe's displaced persons -- a significant number of whom eventually settled in the Kansas City area -- but also for his decision in 1948 to extend de facto recognition to the infant state of Israel.

In that decision, two prominent members of the Kansas City Jewish community — lawyer A.J. Granoff and clothing retailer Eddie Jacobson, Truman's former haberdashery partner — played prominent roles. Even though the Truman-Jacobson downtown Kansas City store failed in the early 1920s, Truman and Jacobson remained close friends.

Ultimately, Truman may have considered himself a professional colleague of the Katz brothers. The teenaged Truman's first job in 1898 had been as a clerk at the Clinton Drug Store on Independence Square. There his duties included dusting cases of patent medicines and noting the prominent Independence residents who, on Sundays, stepped behind a

When Katz Drugs turned 40 in 1954, the 33rd president agreed to a cake-cutting photo op with Ike and Mike in his downtown Kansas City office.

store partition to down a shot of whisky before heading off to church.

According to Chain Store Age, the trade publication that published the "birthday cake" photo of Truman with the Katz brothers in December 1954, the former president "admitted that he wished he had opened a drug store instead of a haberdashery…"

THE WHITE HOUSE
WASHINGTON

July 6, 1945

Dear Mr. Katz:

Thank you for your friendly letter. I appreciate your generous offer to be of service as well as your solicitous interest in my welfare.

The President has had much pleasure in signing one of his photographs for Mr. M. R. Shlensky and I am transmitting it herewith.

With all good wishes,

Very sincerely yours,

MATTHEW J. CONNELLY
Secretary to the President

Although Truman Library files contain little correspondence between the President and the Katz family, in 1945, executive Morris Shlensky requested, and got, a signed photograph.

Continued from page 110)
Katz designers, working from experience, had installed the drawers from the floor up because overhead drawers had made it more difficult to keep track of particular medications. A 7-cubic-foot refrigerator with a "biological insert" of eight drawers provided temperature-controlled storage of vaccines. The prescription counter, with its own neon sign, was placed at the very back of the store.

A WAR BETWEEN KATZ AND MILGRAM WOULD BE DESTRUCTIVE ENOUGH...

This represented the latest in retail design, at least until the next Katz store opened, such as the one on Minnesota Avenue in Kansas City, Kansas, in 1948.

That featured an acoustic room for phonographs, motorboats, and a walk-in humidor for cigars. It had a bigger prescription counter than the one at Linwood and Troost, and an optometrist, and a receptionist for the optometrist.

In the early 1940s, Katz executives began experimenting with a "self-service" concept they introduced to several Kansas City stores.

Morris Shlensky, a Katz vice president, described "streamlined merchandising" during a 1941 speech to the South Central Business Association when the Linwood and Troost store first opened. That location was the 17th in the Katz chain, as well as the fourth "self-serve" store to be opened across Kansas City.

Patrons at a Katz "self-serve" store passed through a turnstile, a fixture more often seen at the ballpark. Customers could freely access and leave the candy and tobacco departments, but no others.

Shopping at some Katz stores meant encountering early examples of features that would become wide-spread, such as acoustic rooms for music, in this case phonographs.

Aware that women and cosmetics were a money-making combination, Katz soon had flourishing cosmetic departments with well-trained saleswomen and special packaging.

In the rest of the store they walked the aisles with a wire basket provided by the store, and the only way out was through the cashier's aisle.

At the same time, Katz executives were thinking about a "super store" concept. By 1946, when the newly expanded store opened at Linwood and Troost, the "self-serve" concept had been abandoned in favor of such "super stores," where the emphasis was on square footage.

The chain's new store in Waldo represented the second largest store at 10,000 square feet. But that would be eclipsed several times over in the next 15 years. The newly renovated store on Minnesota Avenue in Kansas City, Kansas, would offer 25,000 square feet, compared to the 23,000 square feet at the Westport and Main store.

All was an apparent success.

Each Sunday morning a small group of Katz executives gathered at the Westport and Main store to receive the estimates of the previous day's receipts.

In March, 1942, the company reported its largest earnings since 1936. Ten years later Earl Katz, a Katz executive and the son of Isaac, announced that the sales of Katz Drugs had reached a new record.

Unemployment had virtually vanished in Kansas City.

But these were prosperous times, especially in Kansas City and St. Louis, both of which benefited from several World War II production plants. Unemployment had virtually vanished in Kansas City. Just south of the city limits, Pratt and Whitney had built a vast aircraft engine plant. Over in Kansas City, Kansas, a North American Aviation plant produced B-25 bombers.

From 1940 through 1943, defense jobs drew about 40,000 new residents to Kansas City.

About This Photo

A SHOPPING basket from the new self-service stores holds a supply of "cold ones."

A cornucopia of liquor bottles is aimed squarely at Thanksgiving holiday shoppers. An impressive list of imported beer (opposite) includes Asahi, Carta Blanca, Lowenbrau and Guinness.

Nevertheless by 1944, there was actually a labor shortage, prompting Kansas City boosters to organize a "Take a War Job" campaign to avoid a slowdown in war-time production.

THAT CHRISTMAS, ONE OF FIVE MONKEYS SHIPPED TO THE WESTPORT AND MAIN STORE THREW A LATCH ON THEIR CAGE.

In Jackson County, which included Kansas City, a high percentage of war workers were women. About 46 percent of the Pratt and Whitney employees were female, as were more than half of the employees at the Lake City ammunition plant in eastern Jackson County.

That prosperity, relative to the rest of the country, continued in Missouri after the war, when the state's unemployment rate was 3.3 percent, compared to the national level of 4.8 percent. By July 1946, the Katz chain would include 21 stores. That year Earl Katz announced that the sales of Katz Drugs had reached a new record.

The attitude of competing merchants can be imagined.

PRICE WARS

The war-time scarcity of many retail goods didn't appear to bother Katz Drugs. Company buyers acquired what stock they could and employees placed it on the shelves, priced aggressively.

Examples, as reported by one regional trade publication in 1942:

- *one pound of Folgers Coffee: 25 cents.*
- *11 ounces of Post Toasties: 5.5 cents.*
- *a 2-pound box of crackers: 11 cents.*
- *20 ounces of Quaker Oats: 6 cents.*
- *a 5-pound bag of Aristos Flour: 19 cents.*

These, the publication stated, represented "below replacement cost prices."

Say what you want about the taste of Katz beer, and opinions seemed to vary, it was reliable, American made, and the price was hard to beat.

Beginning with Ike, the company's taste in architecture ran to
the modern. Mike Katz (right) and Isaac's son, Earl, look at the scale
model of a new store.

Katz had adopted this policy, the publication speculated, because Milgram, a Kansas City grocery chain, had begun selling drug items below cost.

This was considered dangerous. A war between Katz and Milgram contained within the Kansas City area, would be destructive enough, one publication said. The larger danger was if grocery chains larger than Milgram entered the drug field. If such companies could make drug departments profitable, "they may enter towns where there are not Katz stores and where there is no drastic cut-rate competition."

Throughout the 1940s in several states where Katz operated, lawmakers attempted to regulate such price wars. In Missouri, they failed.

"It looks as though the stage is being set for a return to the dog-eat-dog practices that plagued the Kansas City market for so many years before the beginning of World War II," surmised one trade publication, Midwestern Druggist, in 1948.

"During the war, the scarcity of merchandise and the great increasing spending power of the consumer to a great extent reduced the effectiveness of price cutting." Now, however, "the purchase value of the

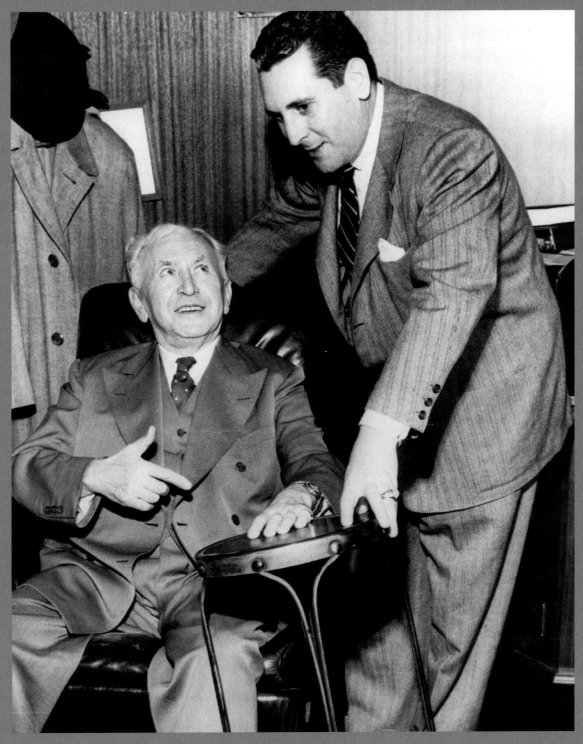

Ike shared an
office with his
son, Earl, and his
comptroller.
It wasn't flashy,
and it was usually
smoke-filled.
Isaac used the
high stool to
sit on and rest
his bad foot.

The company quickly diversified from a normal drug store to a one-stop shopping experience where you could get pantry staples like honey, clothes, athletic equipment, furniture, jewelry, pet supplies, electronics and, of course, what other drug stores had.

dollar is shrinking so rapidly due to the present trend toward inflation, consumers are becoming price-conscious and merchandise at cut-rate prices again has its appeal."

Katz long had advertised a disproportionate number of grocery items at prices that appeared to be below cost, wrote an editor for the St. Louis Interstate Merchant. This, the editor maintained, slyly suggested that all of its merchandise could be counted on to be similarly priced.

"Katz has been a ruthless operator," the publication added. Katz officials could answer that maybe they just worked harder, or longer.

In July 1946, the company announced that the Linwood and Troost store would stay open until midnight, one hour later than most other Katz locations.

UNSTOPPABLE

In December 1946, the 23rd store in the Katz chain opened in the St. Louis suburb of Maplewood. The following March, the

company announced that 23 Katz stores had produced a record volume of business in 1946.

By May 1948, Katz operated 24 stores. That month it announced plans for a store in Independence, the 27th store in the chain, and the 17th in greater Kansas City.

The new store in Memphis opened in September 1954.

That Christmas, one of five monkeys shipped to the Westport and Main store threw a latch on their cage. Employees with fishnets chased the monkeys for hours before securing them.

In March 1956, the company announced a two-year expansion plan, with eight new units planned at a cost of $7 million. That August, sales and net profits for the first six months of that year were declared the largest on record.

That December the 21st store in greater Kansas City opened at 31st Street and Van Brunt Boulevard. It was the chain's 36th store.

On November 9, 1956, founder Isaac Katz died at the age of 77.

LIVING LARGE

Minnie and Isaac cut a figure wherever they went; here, on the sand at the Florida Hollywood Beach hotel.

"ISAAC KATZ WAS FABULOUS."
So read the first line of Isaac's obituary in the Nov. 10, 1956, edition of The Kansas City Star. Another adjective often used to describe him: leonine.

He was, wrote another Star reporter, "probably the most arresting figure in Kansas City — a massive body of a man; rugged, lined faced, topped with a shock of white hair over dark eyebrows...."

ISAAC KATZ'S sense of style was undeniable. His white-haired portrait, paired with that of his brother Mike in so many newspaper ads, presented him as Katz Drugs' George Washington to his brother's John Adams. His squared shoulders, combined with his hesitant walk and ever-present cane lent him an air of gravitas, except for the times when he was funny and self-deprecating, which he often was.

Star reporters in search of lively copy rarely left Katz's desk disappointed. There was the time in 1933 when he and Minnie, touring the Mediterranean and North Africa, discovered that a bank holiday in the United States had devalued their currency.

Katz cabled the company offices in Kansas City: "Paris or home?"

The reply was "Paris," but Katz came home anyway.

"It was a bright sunny day in Egypt," Katz explained later. "Everything [was] normal in Cairo that morning, the heavy normalcy of Egyptian centuries …

> "HE CONVERTED THE CORNER DRUG STORE INTO A MAX REINHARDT SPECTACLE —
> ALL WITHOUT KNOWING THE DIFFERENCE BETWEEN AN ASPIRIN AND A SODA BICARBONATE…"
> — A 1935 ARTICLE

I had seen misery — stark depressing pauperism, under nine flags. And there the American dollar was suddenly four bits on land and not more than six bits, Italian money, on boat.

"I came home, to Kansas City."

Many reporters enjoyed Katz's gift for show business. A 1935 article described him as the "David Belasco of the retail drug business," alluding to a theatrical producer of the time — and then compared him to another showman.

"[Katz converted] the mildly profitable, modest and wholly ethical corner drug store into a glittering three-ring circus, a Max Reinhardt spectacle -- all without knowing, in the early days at least, the difference between an aspirin and a soda bicarbonate…"

"Ike, the impresario, put on breathless Million Dollar Sales, took 12 full-page ads in The Star, gave away raincoats, eggs and subscriptions to magazines, hired Convention Hall for Katz jamborees, and generally managed to have his

methods despised and disparaged by his competitor, while the citizens, charmed by the uproar, blocked traffic trying to get in his stores.

"If his already appalling drug stores develop into more colossal, super-productions, it will be Ike Katz, the old maestro, who directs the show, lines up the dancing girls and the elephants, and keeps the crowd moving towards the big tent."

In 1942, early in World War II, when Americans were being asked to exercise restraint for the duration, Isaac Katz donated his seven-passenger Packard to the Kansas City chapter of the American Red Cross. Even in simplifying, Isaac Katz went big.

That didn't mean war-time prevented him from seeing opportunity. When nylon stockings grew scarce early in the war, Katz Drug pulled 2,000 pairs off its shelves.

The Isaac Katz's were in their element at fine hotels, including later, the Arizona Biltmore, and on board a cruise liner.

Later when the company had trouble getting merchandise, Katz sent executive Morris Shlensky to New York with a supply of those stockings.

A half-dozen pairs for the executives' wives usually worked nicely, and the merchandise was soon on the shelves.

How frustrating it must have been for competing drug chains that often were forced to match Katz Drugs prices, but never could compete with Isaac Katz's cult of personality.

Photographers routinely found him with the famous, such as Jack Dempsey. (Katz gave a 1940 dinner in Florida for the former heavyweight champ.) He palled around with mezzo-soprano Nan Merriman and singer Morton Downey during the 1948 Katz Kansas City Philharmonic concert, and soprano Rose Bampton and tenor Lauritz Melchior at the 1950 concert. A trip to Los Angeles to enroll a daughter at the University of Southern California included a visit with Carl Laemmle,

> "HE HAD HIS SUIT COATS TAILORED WITH EXTRA LARGE POCKETS, ALLOWING HIM TO PASS OUT GUM, CANDY AND PERFUME TO PEOPLE ALONG THE WAY. HE WAS A REGULAR 'PIED PIPER.'"
> — STEVE KATZ

chief executive at Universal Pictures, to which a photographer was invited.

He wasn't always expansive. Steve Katz tells a story that he says typifies the way his Grandfather thought: "He was attending the National Association of Chain Drug Stores meeting where, by surprise, he was called upon to speak. He stood and said, 'As Antony said to Cleopatra one moonlight night on the Nile, I didn't come here to talk.'"

Even his bad foot seemed part of the package. During the 1940s, a specialist spoke to Katz about the possibility of having it corrected. Katz's personal physician thought it a bad idea. "Leave Ike Katz alone," he said. "After all these years that bad foot is part of him.

"He wouldn't be Ike Katz without it."

Later in life, Ike Katz would have his driver let him out of the car several blocks from his 12th and Walnut office so he could walk. He had his suit coats tailored with extra large pockets, allowing him to pass out gum, candy and perfume to people along the way. "He was a regular 'pied piper,' " his grandson says.

According to one story, on a trip to Florida, Katz brought enough sample boxes that he booked a separate hotel room for it all.

He held court.

At the annual Philharmonic concerts in Kansas City's Municipal Auditorium, he routinely reserved several boxes along the auditorium's west grandstand while Michael did the same on the east side.

"There's Ike over there," Mike said to a Star reporter, pointing across the hall. "See how my brother and I work this thing? He has his side and I have mine.

"We never trespass on each other."

In the 1950s, visitors to his office found Isaac Katz in a maroon leather chair given him for his 70th birthday by his company's

Isaac Katz, at his desk in a 1949 photo, had laser focus before there were lasers, interest in people and intellectual curiosity about almost everything.

directors. It was, he noted, the kind of chair used by Supreme Court justices. Then he would wax wise. Maybe it was a good thing that he had hurt his foot, he sometimes said. That meant he had spent more time thinking than playing.

Visitors also would have been treated to Ike's sense of humor. Usually displayed somewhere was a sign with the headline "Time Allowed For Interviews During Business Hours In This Establishment" (facing page). Under "Ike's Rules," for example, life insurance agents got 1 second, friends wanting to borrow $5 got 3 seconds, but friends who ask us to lunch got 60 minutes.

If larger than life to the regular public, Isaac also was that to members of his own family.

Steve Katz, grandson of Ike, remembers his Saturday visits to the Katz corporate offices at 12th and Walnut streets in downtown Kansas City.

"The office was always filled with cigar smoke," Katz once wrote in The Kansas

> "HE WAS PROBABLY THE MOST ARRESTING FIGURE IN KANSAS CITY."
> — THE KANSAS CITY STAR

City Star. "When Grandpa was not smoking a cigar he was chewing one. He kept a brass spittoon by his desk."

He and Minnie's home in ritzy Mission Hills, Kansas, was well-known for its swimming pool, artificial pond, automatic lawn watering system and pipe organ. Its gardens were an attraction on the homes tours of the day.

Isaac apparently never forgot his own beginnings as a news butcher on the railroad. He developed a friendship with Johnnie Dukie, a Kansas City Star newsboy who worked the corner of 12th and Walnut.

Dukie, Steve Katz said, had a standing order to deliver copies of The Star to the Katz offices.

While Ike and Dukie shared a newsboy background, it's also possible that Ike — who used a cane in his later years to accommodate his bad foot — felt a kinship with Dukie, who wore leg braces, a legacy of his bout with polio.

Decades before the term was coined, Isaac Katz lived large.

He explained it this way to the Associated Press in 1954: "If you operate in a big way, you can't live small."

He lived that way until the end. On Saturday, Nov. 3, 1956, Isaac and Michael Katz were photographed with soprano Jean Fenn and tenor Jan Peerce at the annual Katz Kansas City Philharmonic concert. The following Monday he suffered a heart attack at his office; he died Nov. 9 at Menorah hospital.

He was 77.

At Katz's funeral, Rabbi Gershon Hadas approved of the use of the word "fabulous" in The Star's obituary.

"This is literally true," Hadas said.

"He was not like most older people," he added. "A survivor; he kept abreast of the times; he was a participant in all that was happening far more than most young people."

TIME ALLOWED FOR INTERVIEWS DURING BUSINESS HOURS IN THIS ESTABLISHMENT

	HRS.	MIN.	SEC.
Friendly Calls	..	2	..
Friendly Calls (when busy)	..	1	..
Life insurance agents	..	..	1
Book agents	..	..	2
Friends with a great scheme	..	..	5
Friends willing to let us in on the ground floor	..	..	..
Friends with a sure winner	..	..	1
Friends who wants us to go fishing	8	1	42
Friends who ask us to drink	?	..	..
Friends who ask us to lunch	..	60	..
Friends wanting to borrow $5.	..	..	3
Friends wanting to borrow $10.	..	..	2
Friends wanting to borrow $100	..	..	1
Collectors (we remit by mail)	..	..	0
Bores – Male	..	..	0
Bores – Female	..	..	6
Bores – Female (if attractive)	..	..	58
Advertising solicitors	..	..	1
Those wanting to pay old bills	16	8	20
Persons wishing us to do work for them	23	59	60

Isaac Katz

KATZ DRUG COMPANY

*There are as many tomorrows
as there were yesterdays.*

— ISAAC KATZ

1950s-1960s

THE MOLD BREAKS

Something is wrong. Revenues break records, but profits are going south. And around every corner is a big-box discounter who doesn't give a fig for personal service.

ON DEC. 31, 1967, Katz Drug closed the doors of its store at 12th and McGee streets in downtown Kansas City.

As Katz battled to increase sales during the 1960s, it closed several smaller stores. But 12th and McGee had been the first store, the former confectionery and cigar store that Isaac and Mike Katz operated after they shut down their businesses in the West Bottoms in 1914.

Earl Katz, Isaac's son, who had grown up working at the store — sometimes standing on a box to operate a cash register when he was a boy — said the company wanted to both acknowledge the past and anticipate the future. The 5,000-square-foot store, he said, although remodeled several times over the years, would never approach the volume and profitability of the more modern Katz locations, which ranged from 25,000 to 50,000 and sometimes even 75,000 square feet.

LOOKING BACK, GOING FORWARD

The closing, Earl said, represented "the passing of an era, and changing trends. From a sentimental point of view, we look with great sadness upon the closing of 12th and McGee."

But, Earl added, "we feel the future is far more exciting and challenging. As my father often said, there are as many tomorrows as there were yesterdays."

But at the Katz Drug Company of the late 1960s, the tomorrows were dwindling down.

1957

Katz sales reach
all-time high of
$44,894,180,
with 38 stores in
Kansas, Missouri,
Iowa, Tennessee
and Oklahoma.

1958

Lunch-counter
sit-in at Katz store
in Oklahoma City
attracts national
attention.

1961

Katz operates 40
stores in five states,
now called Katz
Drug Company
Discount Super
Stores instead of
Katz Cut-Rate
Super Drug Stores.

**When the Kansas City Philharmonic
asked Isaac for a donation,
he saw an opportunity to give the
city an annual free concert, which
Katz then sponsored for more than
25 years. Above, Earl Katz and
Morris Shlensky talk with headliner
Victor Borge.**

As the executives of Katz Drug navigated forward through the mid-1950s and 1960s, they maintained their ties with the company's past, continuing to invest in saturation advertising, emphasizing cut-rate prices and sponsoring the annual Kansas City Philharmonic concerts with headline stars such as Eddie Fisher, Edie Adams, Louis Armstrong and Liza Minnelli.

But they also did their best to respond to an evolving retail marketplace.

Company execs long had recognized the need for larger stores — in the late 1950s Katz had shut down the company's second location at 8th Street and Grand Avenue.

As the company claimed in its 1960 annual report: "Units of ever-increasing size were erected to offer dual inducement — huge assortment and discount prices."

From 1956 through 1960 the company added 11 "giant" stores, representing a total of 348,500 square feet of retail space. The Katz concept: "super size" installations that offered perhaps 50,000 items over an equal amount of square footage, that promoted one-stop shopping and correspondingly boosted volume and profits.

Internal Katz Drug documents archived at the State Historical Society of Missouri Research Center – Kansas City suggest just how scientific the engineering of the impulse purchase had become by the 1960s, and how much Katz executives sweated the details and often were their own worst critics.

They believed with reason that they were dominating their territory.

In the early 1960s, Marvin Katz, son of Michael and company promotions director, pitched the Katz Drug chain as a reliable test market option to the Pyrex Division of the Corning Glass Co. In a letter to Pyrex, Marvin Katz claimed that while the company operated 38 stores in only 10 counties, in those 10 counties the company accounted for 24 percent of the total retail drug volume.

Another claim: that in just the three-county area of greater Kansas City — an area in which Katz operated 20 drug stores out of 401, or just under five percent — it handled 42 percent of the region's retail drug volume.

(Continued on page 138)

Every year audience members got a handsome, ad-strewn program. Headlining artists, as in the list above, were top tier.

A GIFT TO THE CITY

FOR MORE THAN 25 YEARS, from 1944 through to its 1971 merger with Skaggs, the Katz Drug Company sponsored an annual fall concert of the Kansas City Philharmonic.

It was high-profile sponsorship of the high-brow, bringing often serious music within reach of anyone who could go to a Kansas City Katz store and ask for a free ticket or receive one in exchange for a purchase as minimal as 50 cents.

Every year, the Kansas City Philharmonic performed with a headlining star at Kansas City's Municipal Auditorium. Katz customers saw performers from the worlds of opera (Rise Sevens in 1946, Lily Pons in 1957); jazz (Louis Armstrong in 1964); swing (Benny Goodman in 1945); pop (Kay Starr in 1955, Connie Francis in 1961, Edie Adams in 1963, Liza Minnelli in 1969 and Pearl Bailey in 1971); champagne music (Lawrence Welk, 1970) and comedy (Jimmy Durante in 1965 and Alan King in 1967).

Group photos were de rigueur. Above, Debbie Reynolds sits between Mike and Ike, Eddie Fisher is on the floor below.

Some performers generated teen idolatry. Teenagers knocked Eddie Fisher to the sidewalk outside his downtown Kansas City hotel in 1954, and Pat Boone needed an escort to exit the auditorium in 1959.

But it was Benny Goodman in 1945 who needed what The Kansas City Star called a "flying wedge of husky auditorium employees to escape the

auditorium, aided by a disguise achieved by taking off his glasses and wearing a hat low over his eyes."

The sponsorship began when supporters of the Kansas City Philharmonic asked Isaac Katz for a $5,000 donation.

"I don't like music quite that much," he said.

But he struck a deal with the orchestra that it would play a concert just for his family and friends. To Isaac Katz, his circle of friends included customers of Katz Drug.

It was not the Katz brothers' first sponsorship of the orchestra. H. F. McElroy, city manager of Kansas City, asked the brothers to sponsor a series of five orchestra concerts in the then-new Municipal Auditorium in the winter of 1937.

For the first show in January, about 5,000 people braved an ice storm to hear a program that featured both Johann Strauss and Duke Ellington. Over five shows, about 30,000 Kansas

City Katz customers heard the Philharmonic.

Perhaps a light went on. That November the company hired bandleader Paul Whiteman to perform at its "party" celebrating its annual Million Dollar Sale. Several thousand were in line when the auditorium doors opened at 7 p.m.

That started its own tradition — popular bandleaders in Municipal Auditorium, sponsored every year by Katz from the late 1930s through the early 1940s. They included bands led by Jimmy Joy, Joe Sanders and Gus Arnheim.

Sometimes dancers also were featured. There was a master of ceremonies, who sometimes told jokes.

Then, in 1944, the company began its Philharmonic sponsorship with a concert featuring pianist Oscar Levant.

The next year Benny Goodman, with Metropolitan Opera mezzo soprano Gladys Swarthout, attracted 20,000 to two shows.

"The Katz Drug company developed a volume business and its organization grew in depth, but never lost

People arrived early for a Katz concert, and it wasn't a stretch to say that Municipal Auditorium was packed to the rafters.

Over the decades, Katz concerts featured headliners such as Jack Benny and Liza Minelli (above), recording artist Kay Starr, diva Lily Pons, singer Pat Boone, and pianist, composer and wit Oscar Levant.

its characteristic showmanship," wrote an unnamed Kansas City Star reporter after the 1945 Goodman-Swarthout performances.

"Its autumn parties that began in the early 1930s became a unique institution. They stepped up

into vaudeville and dance bands, often with better names as drawing cards.

"It was a proud year when girthy Paul Whiteman and his band were featured.

"Last year the Katz management tried an experiment that was at once a friendly gesture toward

**Above left, Louis Armstrong and Kansas City
Philharmonic conductor Hans Schwieger are flanked by
Earl Katz and Morris Shlensky. Above right,
headliner Jimmy Durante.**

the present-day Philharmonic organization, and
a test of how wide a response a program of other
than light music would draw.

"Oscar Levant was tossed in for good measure and
there was not space for the responding throng."

Isaac Katz considered it money well spent.

"After all, you know, the people of Kansas City
have done a lot for us," he told a Kansas City
reporter in January 1937, just before the first of
the company's sponsored Philharmonic concerts.

"Why shouldn't we show our appreciation?"

1961

Opens largest store, 70,000-square-foot Katz Discount City, in Springfield, Missouri. Its first store in the chain not to include "Drug" in the name.

1962

Michael Katz dies Jan. 8, age 74.

1962

Wal-mart opens its first store in Rogers, Ark.

The company believed in the value of employee recognition. A 5-year pin was something to work for and keep.

(Continued from page 133)

That wasn't all. Katz maintained that the company enjoyed the largest average per-store volume of any drug chain in the country, more than $1.3 million a year.

Marvin Katz wasn't exaggerating. The company would be able to report plenty of profits to its shareholders in the 1960s.

Its performance during 1964 bettered that of any year in Katz history, with sales for the 12-month period increasing 7.5 percent from the year before, with $55+ million in gross revenues compared to $51+ million in 1963.

That was unprecedented — at least until the following year, 1965, when the company reported sales of more than $64 million, a 15 percent increase from the year before.

What company officials called the largest drug store in the world opened in Topeka in September 1960. The next year another 50,000-square-foot store opened in Florissant, a St. Louis suburb.

EMPLOYEES WERE CRUCIAL

Katz Drug was the last of the "service-type" operations, with trained personnel running individual departments such as cosmetics or hardware or sporting goods.

"Self-selection where practical, personal service where needed," the company's 1963 annual report said.

Company officials were alert to the growth of large self-service discounters who did not always put the same premium on sales personnel as did Katz. But the floor sales associate was crucial to a Katz store's volume.

"Clerks must know what to do and say, and must be sufficiently motivated to achieve results," read the same 1963 annual report.

"Katz conducts a continuous program of personnel training aimed at increasing and upgrading sales. For example, clerks are carefully trained to sell the customer a larger size of an item, to sell a second or spare item, to sell a related item, and to sell an additional item. In addition to morale-building through training sessions, Katz personnel are also motivated to greater productivity by interesting contests and price-incentive programs."

The Katz executives succeeded. In 1971, when they decided to sell the company, Katz operated about 65 stores, including a number of separate leased departments within larger stores operated by other companies. The company had an annual sales volume of more than $100 million in a competitive market.

But from the mid-1950s through the 1960s the company also had to confront a number of setbacks, challenges and apparent missteps.

Among them:

■ The death of Michael Katz. The passing of the younger Katz Drug co-founder in January 1962, left the company without its last link to its earliest days. The company went forward with Earl Katz, son of Isaac, as well as such non-family leadership as Morris Shlensky, a veteran company executive.

■ Civil rights. Katz Drug executives appeared slow to recognize and address evolving public accommodations policies in the Midwest. Even after a Des Moines store manager in 1948 was convicted of violating a state civil rights law, company execs in 1958 apparently were caught unaware when young members of the Oklahoma City branch of the National Association for the Advancement of Colored People organized a sit-in over several days at a Katz Drug lunch counter.

Today the Katz Drug sit-in remains a landmark event in the civil rights history of Oklahoma.

■ Missouri Sunday sales law. A new state Sunday sales law, upheld by the Missouri Supreme Court in 1963, enshrined a legal barrier to achieving more volume — by taking one day off the Katz sales calendar each week. In 1962 Katz Drug would omit a quarterly dividend for the first time since 1938, attributing the slowdown at least in part to the confusion surrounding the Missouri Sunday sales law.

■ Federal perjury indictment. In December 1963, a federal grand jury in Kansas City indicted Morris Shlensky, then Katz Drug president, on a perjury charge concerning

This Katz manager's badge, probably made of brass, is most likely from the 1920s, as evidenced by the vintage logo.

MISS BRADFIELD

A Mid-Century Modern ('50s) cat welcomes
customers to a Katz location with a cafeteria
just inside the door.

As more discount and chain stores opened in a territory, the revenue pie got sliced thinner and thinner.

payoffs he allegedly made to Teamster union officials in an effort to maintain favorable contract terms. A jury acquitted Shlensky of the charge the following spring.

■ Constant pressure to maintain market share and increase sales. Ultimately, every year, this continued to be the company's most pressing challenge.

A THINNER SLICE
In 1963, Frank Hoffman, a Katz supervisor in charge of the chain's electrical and hardware department, traveled to Cleveland to address officials of the Cole National Corporation, a key manufacturing company.

Hoffman described to them a retail "profit squeeze," which he was sure his listeners already had noticed.

"Discount stores and chain stores, our own and others, are opening up at an extremely rapid rate," Hoffman said.

"All we're doing is taking a pie and slicing it up a little bit thinner. We don't know, necessarily, that there are that many more dollars in a particular market, but all this has done is spread it around a little bit more."

Throughout the 1950s and

1963

The Kansas City Chiefs play their first game.

1964

Kansas City voters approve public accommodations ordinance, which bans segregation in public places.

Miss Swearengin's badge has the updated "Katz Super Stores" logo that the company used in the '50s.

1960s, Katz Drug sought to increase sales volume by filling more square footage with merchandise, on the theory that ever-larger volume on discount-priced goods would, in turn, deliver bigger profits.

Accordingly, in 1961, the chain opened its biggest store ever, with 75,000 square feet, in Springfield, Missouri.

The store, called Katz Discount City, was the first Katz location without the word "drug" in its name. But other rival chains, such as Fan Fair department stores, already were where Katz was only still going, building even bigger stores, such as three 100,000-square-foot stores in the Denver, Colorado, area in the early 1960s.

One solution: leased departments within those stores, which Katz Drug did negotiate beginning in 1961 in those three Denver area Fan Fair stores.

Throughout the late 1950s and 1960s, the company still managed to respond to most challenges and post ever-larger sales figures.

And yet it seemed as if the degree of difficulty always was increasing.

Earl Katz, in a February 1958 notice to employees, explained that margins had been decreasing and urged even greater fidelity to the company's core sales ethic. While the 1957 sales year produced the highest sales volume in Katz Drug history, he said, this had not been true of profit. The lower amount of gross profit, he added, resulted from "keen competition from other drug chains, super markets, variety stores, discount houses and department stores."

> **"THERE ARE AS MANY TOMORROWS AS THERE WERE YESTERDAYS."**
> **— ISAAC KATZ**

That, coupled with the rising costs of doing business, such as higher wages and transportation charges, made ever-bigger profits more challenging to achieve.

"Your help and support are needed to overcome our many problems," he wrote.

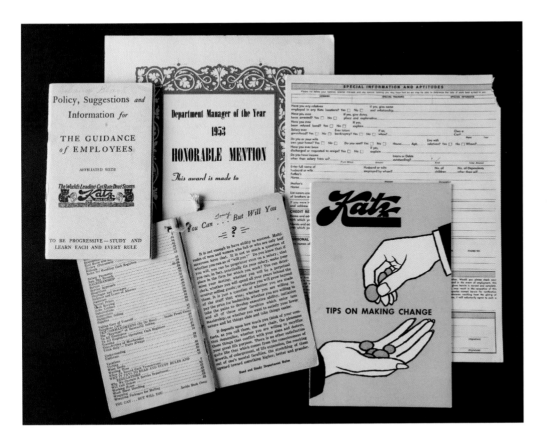

It would have been hard for a Katz employee to say she wasn't given adequate training or the opportunity for recognition.

Morris Shlensky, in a similar note the next month, seconded the motion.

"Those who are responsible for selling should realize the important role they play in our operations," he wrote. "Merely waiting on people is a service that lacks the excitement as well as the profit that can be developed in every transaction.

"There can be an exhilaration and a satisfaction if each and every one of you will say — 'What can I do to increase the sale?' — This self-motivation will bring new thrills to you as a salesperson and will make you a far more valuable employee to us."

But after the January 1962 death of Michael Katz it would have been reasonable for some Katz Drug execs and associates to wonder: Is this how Ike and Mike would have done it? *(Continued on page 149)*

THIS HANDBOOK, apparently distributed to employees in the 1930s, covered the basics of retail sales.

But Katz executives seemed also to believe that the best employees brought both their hearts and minds to the workplace. The handbook included a "Ten Commandments" of living and working, authored "By The Boss" — presumably Isaac Katz. "Mind your own business and in time you will have a business of your own to mind," read one example.

The handbook offered directions on avoiding sloth, and also warned of the dangers of "the easy chair, the pleasures that demoralize," lest such habits allow the employee to become a "perpetual clerk." Other advice found under "You Can…But Will You?" suggested that hard work was its own reward and fidelity to the company's goals could bring personal satisfaction and even enrichment, given that an employee's hard work likely would be recognized and rewarded.

If new Katz employees wondered how seriously such rules were taken by management, they could simply observe Isaac and Michael Katz, famous for coming early and staying late.

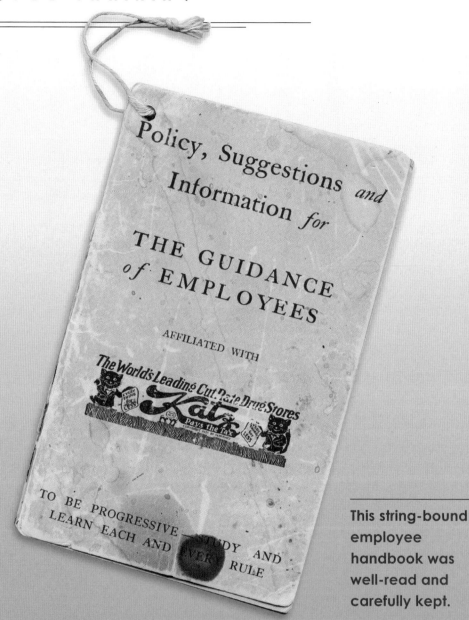

This string-bound employee handbook was well-read and carefully kept.

TEN COMMANDMENTS

(By The Boss)

1. Don't lie. It wastes my time and yours. I'm sure to catch you in the end, and that's the wrong end.

2. Watch your work, not the clock. A long day's work makes a long day short, and a short day's work makes my face long.

3. You owe so much to yourself that you can't afford to owe anybody else. Keep out of debt or out of my store.

4. Give me more than I expect, and I will give you more than you expect; increase my profit and I will increase your pay.

5. Dishonesty is never an accident. Good men, like good women, can see temptation when they meet it.

6. Mind your own business, and in time you will have a business of your own to mind.

7. Don't do anything to hurt your self-respect. The employee who is willing to steal for me is capable of stealing from me.

8. It's none of my business what you do at night, but if dissipation affects what you do next day and you do half as much, you'll last half as long.

9. Don't tell me what I like to hear, but what I ought to hear. I don't need a valet to my vanity, but I need one for my money.

10. Don't kick if I kick; if you're worth while correcting, you're worth while keeping. I don't waste time cutting specks out of rotten apples.

Policy, Suggestions *and* Information *for*

THE GUIDANCE *of* EMPLOYEES

AFFILIATED WITH

The World's Leading & Cut Rate Drug Stores
Katz
Pays the Tax

A deposit of fifty cents will be required on this manual. This amount will be refunded when the holder leaves the organization if manual is returned.

TO BE PROGRESSIVE — STUDY AND LEARN EACH AND EVERY RULE

---

another salesperson. If you are not sure whether the customer is being served by anyone, because the salesperson may for the moment have stepped aside to get merchandise or change, use "Are you being waited upon?" or "Is someone helping you?"

Personal Approach: Used where the customer is known by name. "Good morning, Mr. Jones." Follow this with one of the above approaches.

Avoid such approaches as "Did you want something?", "Something for you?", "What's yours?", "Who's next?", "Yes, Ma'am", "Are you getting yours", and "Something in tooth paste?"

Arguing with Customers: The utmost courtesy is to be shown to each customer, whether it is returned or not. Arguments of any nature are to be avoided at all times. Remember, THE CUSTOMER IS ALWAYS RIGHT, and it is our policy to go to the extreme in order to adjust matters to the customer's entire satisfaction, rather than our own.

Better Salesmanship:

Resolved:

I will enter my department each morning with a smile.

I will not "high-hat" my customers.

I will not address customer "brother" or "dearie."

I will not correct my customer's pronunciation.

I will sell, not argue.

I will not ignore customers who come to my department during the last half hour of the business day.

I will keep my department as orderly as possible.

When my department is busy, I will endeavor to serve two or more people at once and keep them both happy.

I will not say "and now, what else," but will try to make a real selling suggestion.

I will do the same kind of selling job in this store

—50—

---

as I would if it were my store with my money invested.

When extra help is brought into my department, I will try to be helpful to them.

I will keep accurate Lost Sale Reports and turn them in, in accordance with the Store Policy.

I will keep well informed on the goods in my department; their quality, fashion, etc.

I will read the advertisements of my store each day and will look at the display windows often.

I will try to remember the old adage, "He serves best who sells most, and he sells most who serves best."

Condensed Rules of Retail Selling: Remember, THE CUSTOMER IS ALWAYS RIGHT. If you keep that idea in mind, fewer disputes will arise and those that do, will be settled with little difficulty. Remember, your customer does not have to trade at our stores and you should honor him the same as you would a guest in your home.

A salesperson to be successful must know his stock. You are expected to familiarize yourself with the merchandise you are selling, its location in the store, its price and one or two "selling hints" concerning it.

Study your "Selling Hints" furnished you by the Buying Department. Your knowledge of merchandise should include a knowledge of a companionate item for practically every item you sell; for instance, tobacco with pipe, rouge with powder, etc.

Give your customer your full attention. Do not look out the door or "around" him or her while you are talking. Give every customer exactly what he or she asks for. Do not attempt to substitute any item for the one requested. You may sell something to go with it, or you may suggest some possible additional want, but be very careful to avoid any suggestion of substitution.

In addressing patrons of our stores, always use the

—51—

---

partments, such as Mail Order, Commissary, Maintenance, Warehouse and Sign Shop.

Salespeople, Non-Salespeople, Department Managers, Floormen, Assistant Managers, and Managers are a part of the Operations Division. The Operations Division is so designed that it works through the Personnel Director and Operation Manager, who report direct to the General Manager.

This Division represents the Management to the Stores and Departments, which are in this classification, and in turn represents the Stores and Departments to the Management.

Merchandising: The Merchandising Division selects and purchases all merchandise and is entirely responsible for the cost and selling price.

At the head of the Merchandising Division is the Merchandising Manager, who reports direct to the General Manager. All buying and advertising is supervised and co-ordinated by the Merchandising Manager, to whom the Head Buyer and Advertising Manager report. The Buyers, who do the direct buying for their departments, report to the Head Buyer. The Advertising Manager is in direct charge of the Advertising Department, layouts, etc.

Salespeople naturally represent a vital part of this Division, since they are responsible for selling merchandise; however, they report directly to their Store Manager.

HISTORY

The Katz Drug Company started in 1914, and opened two small stores; one at Eighth and Grand and another at Twelfth and McGee. Business prospered only to a small degree, and in 1917, the Katz Brothers conceived the idea of getting more business and taking smaller profit. They thought by selling Standard, Nationally Advertised brands of merchandise at cut prices, their purpose would be fulfilled. This plan succeeded to the degree that the growth of the business has been phenomenal.

—6—

The public was quick to realize the wonderful savings to be made, due to low prices and exceptional service. It was, therefore, necessary to enlarge the original two stores and to add additional stores, until now the Katz Drug Company is one of the largest and most successful Retail Drug Chains in the country. At the present time, we are operating five stores in Kansas City, Missouri, one in Kansas City, Kansas, one in St. Joseph, Missouri, and one in Des Moines, Iowa. We carry over 25,000 items and employ over 600 people in our great organization.

This growth has only been possible, due to the faithful carrying out of the Policy, of Mr. Isaac Katz and Mr. M. H. Katz, which was adopted in 1917. This policy was to give the public what they wanted, plus courteous treatment, prompt service, and at the lowest possible price.

CO-OPERATION

Most people look upon co-operation as a sentiment, where as a matter of fact, it is an absolute business necessity. The Line of Organization of Katz Drug Company, and the duties involved are very distinct, and its success depends upon co-operation. It is, therefore, necessary that all divisions co-operate with each other and that each and every member of the entire organization co-operate in every respect. The "Key Word" of all employees is to be "Co-Operate At All Times."

REPUTATION

The Katz Drug Company's reputation and advertising brings our customers to our stores. This reputation, which has been justly earned, is Right Merchandise, Right Price, and Right Service, also, that we give customers what they ask for and never substitute. It is the service that satisfies that brings the many thousands of customers to our stores daily.

—7—

You Can *Tony* . . . But Will You

=== ? ===

It is not enough to have ability to succeed. Multitudes of men and women who fail or who are only half successes have that. It is not so much a question of whether you can as of "will you?" Do you know that if you will, you can be proprietor even on a salary; that you can, in fact, practically fix your salary, make your place in the firm for which you work? You can determine your destiny, whether you will be a perpetual clerk, whether you will spend all your years behind the counter selling goods; or whether you will grow beyond these. It is just a question of whether you are made of the stuff that wins; whether you are willing to pay the price for leadership, whether you are willing to take the pains to develop executive ability, initiative and all of those other faculties which enter into mastership; or whether you want to satisfy your lower nature and let things slide and take things easier.

It depends upon how much you think of your comforts, as you call them, the easy chair, the pleasures that demoralize, whether you are willing to sacrifice those things that conflict with your aims and desires, your great life purpose. There is no other satisfaction quite like that which comes from the consciousness of growth, of enlargement, of life expansion, the reaching out of one's mental faculties, the stretching of them upward toward something higher, better and grander.

Read and Study Department Rules

BY 1967, corporate instructions for new Katz Drug employees still stressed the importance of a cheery deportment, but also included advice on the mysteries of modern shopping, such as the "charge card" that some customers then were using (although purchases above $25 had to be approved by a store manager).

The instructions also included the advice for employees to respectfully suggest purchases that would either increase store volume or revenues.

Such advice could be given in several separate scenarios, among them "Larger Size," "More Than One," "Better Quality" and "High Profit Items." An example of "High Profit Items" occurred when a customer wanted to buy Bayer aspirin at a minimal profit to the company.

Suggesting the Katz brand aspirin — which was lower in price but represented a bigger profit — would benefit revenues.

EMPLOYEE INDOCTRINATION MANUAL

It is the privilege of the Katz Drug Co. to welcome you as a new employee!

The purpose of this manual is to explain to you some of the policies and procedures you will be expected to follow in your new position. It tells what we expect from you, and what you may expect from us.

We want you to carefully read and understand this manual so that you will know what to do-- and how to do it. If your questions are not answered thoroughly in the following pages, please consult your Store Manager or Assistant Store Manager. They are here to help you.

Revised 10/67

Page 1

What a concept: This instruction regarding use of the new "charge card," below, detailed how customers used such cards to purchase merchandise "for which he or she is billed once each month."

An example of the "More Than One" scenario: Whenever a customer asked for a pack of cigarettes, an employee should "suggest the economy of a carton."

VI.   CASH HANDLING   (Continued)

7.   CUSTOMER RECEIPT - Every customer is to be given a correct receipt for purchases. There are to be no exceptions to this rule.

8.   PROFESSIONAL COURTESY DISCOUNT CARDS - Some members of the Medical Profession will have courtesy discount cards which entitle them to a discount of 10% off the regular price of the merchandise. Exceptions where no discount is given are sale merchandise, beer, soda pop, bottle goods, cigarettes, cigars, food, candy, and items which are priced less than 10% above the cost.

9.   CUSTOMER CHARGE CARD - Many customers have charge cards. No discount is involved, unless used by a Katz employee or in conjunction with a Courtesy Discount Card. The customer then charges merchandise for which he or she is billed once each month. Charge sales $25.00 or over must be approved by Store Management before releasing the merchandise to your customer.

(Note - These two cards - the Courtesy Discount Card and Customer Charge Card - are sometimes confused; therefore, they should be completely understood and distinguished as two different types of cards by you.)

10.   PACKAGE STAPLING - After sacking merchandise, place receipt in the center of the fold at the top of the sack and place one staple through the center of that fold.

Page 9

VI.   CASH HANDLING   (Continued)

11.   CHECK CASHING - Customer may normally give a check for the amount of the purchase (call member of management who must approve the check). Refer payroll checks to the department which is specified to cash payroll checks.

VII.   CUSTOMER SERVICES

1.   SALESMANSHIP - If employed as a salesman, your main function is to serve the customer. Through suggestion, it is often possible to influence the customer to make purchases other than those which they intended to buy. Close each sale with, "Thank you for shopping at Katz".

SUGGEST:

a. Companion items. (Customer buys toothpaste, suggest brush.)

b. Larger size. (Customer asks for 29¢ toothpaste, inform her of savings by buying 77¢ size.)

c. More than one. (Customer asks for a package of cigarettes, suggest the economy of the carton.)

d. Better quality. (Customer asks for York alcohol at 21¢, suggest Chemtest or Squibb at 59¢.)

e. High profit items. (Customer asks for Bayer Aspirin at $1.67 and hardly any profit. Suggest Chemtest Aspirin, Katz private label at 79¢, and a good gross profit.)

Be a real salesman and enjoy your job. Recognize each customer even though you are busy with other customers. They won't mind a short wait if they know you realize they are there. Be pleasant, yet businesslike and you will soon earn the respect and admiration of both customers and fellow employees.

Page 10

Michael Katz, who outlived his hard-charging brother by 5 years, by all accounts had a more collaborative style. An equally canny executive, he was devoted to his family and, in later years, known for his gifts to the community.

(Continued from page 143)

THE YOUNGER BROTHER

One day in 1960, while visiting Los Angeles, Michael Katz walked into a drugstore. Soon he was surrounded by seven store employees, all of whom recognized him because they once had worked for Katz Drug.

By this time, Mike's title was board chairman. His hobby and vocation, for decades, had been the same: walking through drug stores, especially his own. He had done this since his earliest days in Kansas City while operating fruit stands in the city's West Bottoms district.

"In my off hours I used to visit cigar and drug stores, hoping some day I could be a store owner," he once said.

"It was my fondest dream."

It was while walking past other Kansas City drug stores in 1917 that Michael Katz had noticed how competitors were passing along the new one-penny tobacco tax to customers. It wasn't long after that when Mike and Isaac Katz agreed to pay the one-cent tax — "Katz Pays the Tax" — which positioned the two Katz stores as the best place to buy cigars and cigarettes and proved the value of their "fast nickels being better than slow dimes" attitude.

Decades later, Mike's habits were little changed. Each working day he was driven — ever since his 1930 kidnapping, he had a chauffeur — to his downtown office, arriving at about 10 a.m. and leaving by perhaps 4 p.m.

His daughter Charlene Glikbarg remembers how her father's mornings began with a ritual involving a pair of scissors and the morning newspaper.

"He would cut out the advertisements every morning," she said. The advertisements were from Katz and its competitors. The week's prices had to be monitored and for Michael Katz that chore was part of his job description.

Mike Katz began every day at home with the morning paper, cutting out the ads of Katz and its competitors, monitoring prices.

The Katz Springfield, Missouri, store was the chain's biggest when it opened in 1961. Stock included 200 hamsters.

By the early 1960s he was in his early 70s.

With his high-profile brother Isaac gone, Michael Katz was the face of Katz Drug. When singers Pat Boone and Lisa Kirk appeared at the annual Katz Philharmonic concert at Kansas City's Municipal Auditorium in 1959, he met them and posed for photographs.

He was described as the opposite of hard-driving. It was his style to walk though a Katz Drug store and not give orders but make suggestions on how merchandise displays could be improved.

Across Kansas City he had become known as a philanthropist. Children at the Jewish Community Center at 82nd Street and Holmes Road swam in a pool dedicated in his name in 1958.

"I am sort of a gardener," he said that day. "I enjoy working quietly at things and seeing them grow."

In 1961, officers of the University of Missouri-Kansas City announced plans for a new $600,000 pharmacy building on its campus, with half of its cost being picked up by the Katz family and its friends.

One of Michael Katz's last projects was the opening of a new store in Springfield, Missouri, in December 1961.

He died of a heart ailment on January 8, 1962, at age 74.

SPRINGFIELD: EVER BIGGER

Two hundred hamsters. One hundred Norelco speed shavers. Fifteen thousand balloons. One pair of jumbo scissors.

All were in place on December 7, 1961, when Katz Drug opened its biggest store ever, in Springfield, Missouri.

The company that during the 1940s and 1950s had perfected the grand-opening ritual, updated the practice for 1961.

A November 28 internal memo distributed to top executives

KATZ 21ST ANNUAL
SPRING DINNER & DANCE
MUEHLEBACH HOTEL - K.C. MO.
MAY 19, 1965

Katz was a company that fostered
employee traditions. This spring dinner-dance
at the Muehlebach was the 21st annual.

THE photo business was repeat business, as customers brought in film for developing, then returned to pick up prints and more Katz-branded supplies.

12 BULBS **2 for 1** **GUARANTEED FLASHBULBS** **#5 CLASS M**

Katz DRUG CO. CAMERA CENTERS **BLUE SAFETY SPOT**

FLASHBULBS

WITH THE NEW *Rhenium* IGNITER

AMERICA'S FINEST PHOTO FINISHING!

MIRACLE lifetime PRINTS

Katz DRUG CO.

all work guaranteed!

JUMBO PRINTS

AMERICA'S FINEST PHOTO FINISHING

MIRACLE lifetime PRINTS

This new method of processing enables us to give you prints of lifetime permanence and brilliance.

Obtainable Only At

Katz DRUG CO.

26 SUPER DEPTS.

SUPER CAMERA DEPARTMENTS

Album pr

Album

Katz **SUPER CAME**

YOUR NEGATIVES Are Enclosed in This Envelope

s Make Wonderful Photo-Greeting Cards

We can transform any good family snapshot into a distinctive Photo-Greeting Card —at low cost, too. And Greetings made from your own snapshots are so personal! Now—how about yours? Ask for our price list if you don't have one.

SNAPSHOT FOLDERS AVAILABLE TOO
If you prefer to slip your own prints into some of the new Christmas Folders, we can help you out there, too. Quantity prints at attractive prices . . . and handsome folder styles for your selection.

Never has our choice of Photo-Greeting Card sentiments and designs been so broad. It will be easy for you to choose a card that's "just right" for you.

Merry Christmas Happy New Year

Merry Christmas and a Happy New Year

Season's Greetings

Season's Greetings

Season's Greetings

Merry Christmas the Year

10 ASSORTED CARDS
Here's a value in colorful, attractive greeting cards that will make a lasting impression wherever they are sent —remarkably low in cost so that anyone in the family can use them. Pick your favorite shot or negative.

ARE NOT IMPRINTED Check

...d cards with envelopes 98c
...d cards with envelopes 2.39
...cards with envelopes 4.49
...cards with envelopes 7.98
CHARGE FOR USING PRINT...
OF NEGATIVE 50c

described the specially-priced merchandise that would draw customers to the location. That included the Norelco speed shavers, which regularly cost the company $12.48 — but which had been obtained at a special cost of $11.48, and would be on sale for $11.99.

Likewise the hamsters, which cost Katz Drug 75 cents each and would be priced at 84 cents.

The 15,000 balloons, many of which were scheduled to be distributed by the "Kat Man," a person wearing a helmet-like cat mask, cost the company $300 and were part of a $1,449 give-away merchandise budget. (Other items included 6,000 potted plants, 6,000 Katz yardsticks and 10,000 Katz shopping bags to be distributed — according to the memo — to customers on their way out, not their way in.)

Finally, more than 100 full pages of newspaper advertising had been scheduled just in December,

at a cost not yet determined. All media outlets, print and broadcast, had promised "human interest" stories from the opening.

And this didn't include the 16 outdoor billboards, the 52 interior placards placed in Springfield busses, and the buffet dinner at the Grove Steak House for guests whose names had been forwarded to the company by the Springfield Chamber of Commerce — an organization that Katz Drug had joined, with the first dues to be submitted by December 1.

Such was the detail with which Katz executives planned their entry into the southwest Missouri market.

It represented a huge bet for the company. The Springfield store, Michael Katz had said in April 1961, represented "the most ambitious and spectacular venture in its history." It would include a linens department, a photography studio and even a bookshop.

(Continued on page 158)

Potted plants (6,000) were among the give-away items at the Springfield store opening. Others were Katz yardsticks (6,000) and shopping bags (10,000).

PHARMACISTS who had been the source of medicinal alcohol during the 1920s were well positioned to fill a need when Prohibition was repealed.

Accordingly, in Des Moines, Iowa, on April 18, 1933, newspaper reporters recorded that it was Katz Drug that served the first 3.2 beer at 1:55 p.m. to a full room of customers who had been sitting at tables for about a half-hour, waiting for the wholesaler's truck to arrive.

Prohibition's repeal wasn't popular with everyone. In 1934, Nebraska lawmakers considered a proposal to ban liquor from drug stores.

Some state representatives trusted the drug store owners. "We are here to drive out the bootlegger and make a respectable business out of liquor; who is a better person to sell liquor than the druggist?" one lawmaker asked.

Still others suggested that legislators had introduced the proposal in the first place just to keep Katz Drug out of Nebraska.

The same year the Beloit Kansas Gazette scolded readers who might be patronizing Katz stores, as they would be guilty of "helping out one of the

Katz sold whiskey in its own series of fancy ceramic decanters which, once drained, could be refilled. The cats varied (Siamese anyone?) but all were high style, highly glazed felines with corked heads. People who knew their bourbon had choices: Earl's "88" or Ezra Brooks, different proofs. Liquor department employees were easy to spot in their yellow and red vests.

really large liquor dealers in Kansas City."

According to the Gazette, Katz was still operating a wholesale liquor business despite a section in the Missouri liquor law that prohibited wholesalers from also selling liquor retail. The company had agreed to get out of the whole-sale business, the newspaper said.

Isaac Katz at one point had invested in Kentucky bourbon in the barrel, said Steve Katz, Isaac's grandson. Eventually Katz Drug marketed a house brand of bourbon, Earl's 88 — an 88 proof variety named for Steve's father Earl, who served as the company's spirits buyer after Prohibition and went on to lead the company for many years.

The company also contracted with McCormick Distilling in Weston, Missouri, just northwest of Kansas City, to supply Katz brands of vodka and gin.

In 1948, a total of 2,296 Independence, Missouri, residents signed petitions saying they were opposed to the city issuing a license to Katz Drug to sell package liquor.

More than 200 opponents personally attended a city council meeting, along with the head of the city's Ministerial Alliance. The Independence police

For those who didn't know their way around a whiskey sour, Katz had guides. As for wine, they seemingly knew then what studies now tell us: drunk in moderation, it can be beneficial to health.

Definitions..

1 Shot—1 ordinary whiskey glass or about one ounce.
1 Dash—Twenty Drops.
1 Barspoon — ½ Tea-spoon.
1 Pony—¾ Whiskey Glass.
1 Jigger—1½ ounces.

Wines....

Since the beginning of civilization and man has become able to enjoy more than the bare necessities of life, wine has been made.

As knowledge and civilization extended, so extended the industry of wine making into a fine art.

Various districts all over the world developed their own types of wines. It is an undisputed fact, when wine and spirits are used in a judicious way, they are beneficial to health for both old and young. Moderation is essential to our happiness and well being in every indulgence.

The general health and long life in the wine drinking countries shows its use with meals is healthful and more productive of good digestion than the use of icy drinks frequently used.

Drinks....

CONEY ISLE 19
¼ Cream
¼ Absinthe
¼ Curacao
¼ Chartreuse

DIAMOND LIL 20
1/5 Grenadine
1/5 Curacao
1/5 Rum
1/5 Absinthe
1/5 Creme de Yvette

FORGET ME NOT 27
1/5 Chartreuse
1/5 Maraschino
1/5 Brandy
1/5 Cream
1/5 Curacao

for the Ages..

ASTORIA QUEEN 90
¼ Jigger Cream
¼ Jigger Maraschino
¼ Jigger Curacao
¼ Jigger Brandy

SWEET MARIE 92
1/5 Cream
1/5 Benedictine
1/5 Curacao
1/5 Brandy
1/5 Chartreuse

chief reported that the company twice, in 1943 and 1945, had been cited for selling liquor to minors.

The company's lawyer, in turn, said both instances had been mistakes and that one of the underage customers had sported sideburns and a mustache.

Ultimately the council voted against the license, but Katz executives chose to open the new store on Independence Square anyway. Years later they opened another Independence store off Noland Road, the city's principal commercial strip.

By the mid-1960s Katz Drug was one of the leading liquor retailers in Missouri. Bill Glikbarg, then a member of the company's board, remembers how store managers made a point of stocking beer at the very back of the stores.

"This meant customers had to walk to the back to get their beer, increasing the chances they would make an impulse purchase," he said.

The company routinely advertised the low price for its own Katz beer, a six-pack for 79 cents at one point in 1962. After a company board meeting during which members voted to mark some items up to increase profits, the price of beer was one of the first prices raised.

This prompted competing retailers to raise their own prices. Soon, Glikbarg got a call from Arthur Mag, the company's legal counsel and board member. It turned out that Katz's competitors had raised their own beer prices so quickly, and in unison, that federal anti-trust officials suspected some sort of price-fixing.

That hadn't happened at all, Glikbarg said.

"But that's just how closely everyone watched the prices at Katz," he said.

In 1962 it was easy to remember the price for a six-pack of Katz Beer: 79 cents. That's because a radio jingle recorded that year made it almost impossible to forget.

Lots of traffic — hot hot sun
And man I'm thirsty when the day's work's done.
Feels good to get home, take my shoes off and then
Hear the wife say, How 'bout a Katz Beer, Ben?
You bet I would, I'm really dry. Make sure it's Katz—
The only kind I buy.
Mmmm boy that's good, sure hits the spot.
Thing I like, it doesn't cost a lot.
Well about how much?
Six for 79
79 cents is awfully low.
That's the Katz price.
Whaddya know.
Where do you go to get Katz beer?
The Katz super store, you know, the one up here.
Mmmm golden Katz Premium beer.
I sure am glad you like it dear.

A third voice then advised:

Take a tip from Ben's smart wife
A hot tired man likes the comforts of life
When your man comes back home tonight
Serve him Katz beer and treat him right.

Katz Premium beer outsells all other beer in the beverage departments of the 19 Katz super discount stores — 79 cents a six pack, "slightly higher in Kansas."

The Katz philosophy really was "build it and they will come." Earl Katz's 1958 note to employees noted that in that year and the next the company would build four new stores and remodel two others.

(Continued from page 153)

There seemed little margin for error, even though Katz Drug had exhibited a pattern of encountering earnings headwinds and yet responding with strength.

For example, net earnings for the first six months of 1957 had dipped, due to the effects of a strike and the expenses involved in several store openings. A June 1957 strike by retail clerks in the 21 Kansas City area Katz stores had lasted two weeks.

"CLERKS MUST KNOW WHAT TO DO AND SAY ..."
— 1963 ANNUAL REPORT

And yet the 1957 calendar year would eventually produce the highest sales volume in Katz's history, according to the Earl Katz note to employees in early 1958.

He had noted that they had remained optimistic and were building four new stores and remodeling two older stores in 1958 and 1959. In August 1959, the company reported that net profits had increased 22 percent during the first six months of the year.

Sales in 1959 topped the $50 million mark for the first time, achieved without any new units.

And yet there was no end to the competition.

Katz executive Al Diamond, in a November 1961 memo describing the opening of the company's leased department start-ups in Houston, Texas, and Covina, California, listed the competing stores that were close to just the Covina location. (They included "CMA at Anaheim, GEMCO, SCOA (just opened and a mile from the store); Whitefront is to be opened shortly which is 3.5 *Continued on page 165)*

In 1957, the wide expanse of the Roeland Park store sported two cats, waving flags, and an invitation to stop for lunch.

THE MOST FAMILIAR LUNCH COUNTER of the civil rights movement belonged to F. W. Woolworth.

In February 1960, four African-American students sat down at the counter in Greensboro, North Carolina, and were refused service. That prompted several months of protest there and elsewhere, culminating not only in the integration of that particular retail store but new momentum to the civil rights movement across the country.

The Katz Drug chain of Kansas City had announced its own decision to integrate some 18 months before. But it had taken two separate lunch counter incidents in Katz stores to prompt the change.

A JURY FOUND IN GRIFFIN'S FAVOR AND AWARDED HER $1.

In 1948, a Des Moines municipal court jury convicted the manager of the local Katz store of violating the state's civil rights law when he refused lunch counter

Edna Williams attended Fisk University in Tennessee, where she met her future husband, Stanley Griffin, who would become one of Iowa's first black physicians.

service to three African-American customers. In 1949 the Iowa Supreme court upheld the ruling.

In 1958, managers of the Oklahoma City, Oklahoma, Katz Drug store refused service to members of the local NAACP Youth Council led by area history teacher Clara Luper. The group returned the next day.

THE TIMES ARE CHANGING

After two days the store served the customers and, back in Kansas City, a Katz executive announced a new integration policy at the chain's 38 stores in Oklahoma, Missouri, Kansas and Iowa.

But that didn't include the Katz location in Memphis, Tennessee.

Internal collections of newspaper clippings maintained at the Katz Drug offices in Kansas City include published accounts of these events, but little more. Steve Katz, grandson of Isaac Katz and himself a Katz Drug veteran, believes Isaac and his brother Michael had no pronounced views on the civil rights movement before or after the 1958 policy change.

In the Des Moines incident, Edna Griffin, her baby daughter and two friends sat down at the Katz lunch counter on July 7, 1948, to order ice cream. The store refused service.

At the time many of Des Moines' restaurants and other places of public accommodation refused to serve African-Americans. Katz's refusal to serve Griffin, however, and the subsequent conviction of the store manager led to more litigation.

Griffin filed a civil lawsuit seeking $10,000 in damages.

During the trial a lawyer representing Katz Drug said the company was an "unfortunate victim" of the Progressive Party and that Griffin was a professional agitator who had been sent to the store by party officials. Another Des Moines resident who was refused service with Griffin was the Polk County chairman of the Progressive Party, which in 1948 had nominated Iowa native Henry Wallace for president.

THE DRAMA IN DES MOINES FORESHADOWED SIMILAR CIVIL RIGHTS ACTIONS ACROSS THE COUNTRY.

The July 7 visit to the Katz lunch counter had occurred, according to one account, right after a Progressive Party rally.

A jury found in Griffin's favor and awarded her $1.

In December 1949, two Des Moines civil rights attorneys negotiated an agreement which ended Katz's discriminatory policies at the Iowa store.

If Katz Drug executives were slow to recognize the civil rights movement and the public accommodations question that their stores' policies represented, they were not alone.

In December 1958, a group of Kansas City activists, the Community Committee for Social Action, resolved to initiate a boycott of several downtown Kansas City department stores. At the time the stores did not allow African-American customers to be served in their restaurants.

Picketing continued for several months before a settlement opened the restaurants to all.

Katz Drug executives, however, were aware of customs outside the Midwest.

The Katz store that had opened in 1954 in Memphis, Tennessee, had been designed with separate lunch counters for white and African-American customers as well as separate restrooms, remembers Colleen Roberts of Edgerton, Missouri, whose father Peter Morton was a store manager.

Margie Morrison, widow of Lee Morrison, another Memphis store manager, remembers a day during the 1950s when her husband received a telephone call telling him of a planned action by local African-American residents who planned to sit down at the white lunch counter.

Clerks refused service, Morrison remembers, before her husband intervened and served the customers.

Whether the store then was considered integrated remains unclear lo Morrison. But she believes her father's decision to serve the customers likely allowed the Memphis store to avoid the confrontation that occurred in Des Moines and would repeat itself in Oklahoma City.

MEMPHIS STORE MANAGER LEE MORRISON RECEIVED A TELEPHONE CALL TELLING HIM OF A PLANNED ACTION.

In the 1990s the National Museum of American History in Washington, D.C., added a portion of the Greensboro lunch counter to its collection.

Today the downtown Des Moines building that housed the Katz Drug store in 1948 has been renamed for Edna Griffin.

The Iowa Civil Rights Commission and the Drake University Law School in 1998 observed the 50th anniversary of the Katz Drug lunch counter integration with a variety of events, including a re-enactment of the lunch counter episode and a presentation of the oral arguments made by lawyers, including those representing Katz Drug, in the subsequent litigation. The drama in Des Moines, it added, foreshadowed similar civil rights actions across the country.

"Through nonviolent protest and legal action in the courts, the movement ended tolerance of open discrimination in our country and resulted in policies and laws prohibiting racial discrimination," the commission announced.

"It may truly be said that those who opposed the discriminatory denial of service at Katz led the way."

Edna Griffin died in 2000. Four years later officials dedicated the Edna M. Griffin Memorial Bridge in Des Moines.

In Oklahoma City, civil rights champions continue to honor the memory of Clara Luper, who died in June 2011.

In 2000, Oklahoma state officials designated a downtown Oklahoma City street the Clara Luper Corridor as part of a beautification project near the state capitol complex.

Daughter of a laborer and a laundress, Clara Shepard Luper, shown in a 1983 photo, had her masters degree in History Education from the University of Oklahoma when she began teaching high school history.

In this 1961 photo, the soaring roof of the Webster Groves, Missouri, store is framed with cantilevered trusses forming inverted pyramids.

Steady business at the key-making kiosk made it a reliable profit center.

(Continued from page 158)
miles from the store, MORE is 4 miles from the store, Unimark is 10 miles, the Golden Rule is 10 miles."

"We are trying to keep up competitive price and are practically meeting all competition," Diamond wrote.

NO DETAIL TOO SMALL

Continuing to do that required a scientific, strategic approach to retailing in which no detail was too trivial or mundane.

One of Diamond's 85 points had stressed the role of a pegboard at the checkout stands. "As it now stands, we have no special room for the displaying of impulse merchandise and this is a big asset in getting extra volume and profit from traffic," he wrote.

Katz officers also advised the Pyrex division to install pegboard, and were specific down to the inch:

The company will be sure, Marvin Katz informed Pyrex, to install a 5-foot-high sheet of pegboard 63 inches long and 32 inches wide. Items would be displayed upon the pegboard and directly below those particular items would be a supply of the same items in their factory cartons.

Retailing was just as scientific over at the key-making kiosk.

Keys had proved to be a reliable profit center. In 1963, in the company's 41 stores, Katz bought an average of $600 worth of blank keys per store, per year. The retail value of that $600 worth of keys was $1,500, meaning that Katz was generating $900 at each store, every year, just in keys.

"We have quite a reputation as pushers," Frank Hoffman, Katz hardware supervisor, told the Cole National Corporation officers in his 1963 Cleveland speech. "And we push hard. When we see something big, we push real hard.

"When we found a business showing the profits that keys do, we

Cash registers played a big part in the rise of Katz Drugs. First of all, they were busy.

started pushing very hard on this…"

Katz, Hoffman added, made a practice of putting the key machines in heavy-traffic locations including the corners of the housewares, hardware or automotive counters.

"These are areas where a big cash register is ringing constantly all day long," Hoffman said.

Hoffman also, in emphasizing the importance of company sales reps coming to him with specific plans, described just what got him out of bed in the morning.

"What I'm interested in is the turnover of my money," he said,

"How quickly can I turn something over? How quickly can I sell something that I bought and in return get back my investment with a profit?

"This is what I'm interested in."

Despite all this attention to small detail, the way forward still seemed to be all about big stores.

In its 1960 annual report, Katz

described the new units being planned as "immense." The first Katz "super" stores had been about 12,000 square feet, but the Topeka unit then being planned would have 50,000 square feet and stock more than 50,000 items. The Florissant store, in a St. Louis suburb, also would be 50,000 square feet.

All this ambition and success attracted occasional suitors. The

---

"I AM SORT OF A GARDENER."
— MIKE KATZ

---

company entered discussions with Food Giant Markets, a West Coast grocery chain. At the April 1961 shareholders meeting, Morris Shlensky told stockholders that the company had been approached by several retail organizations in recent years.

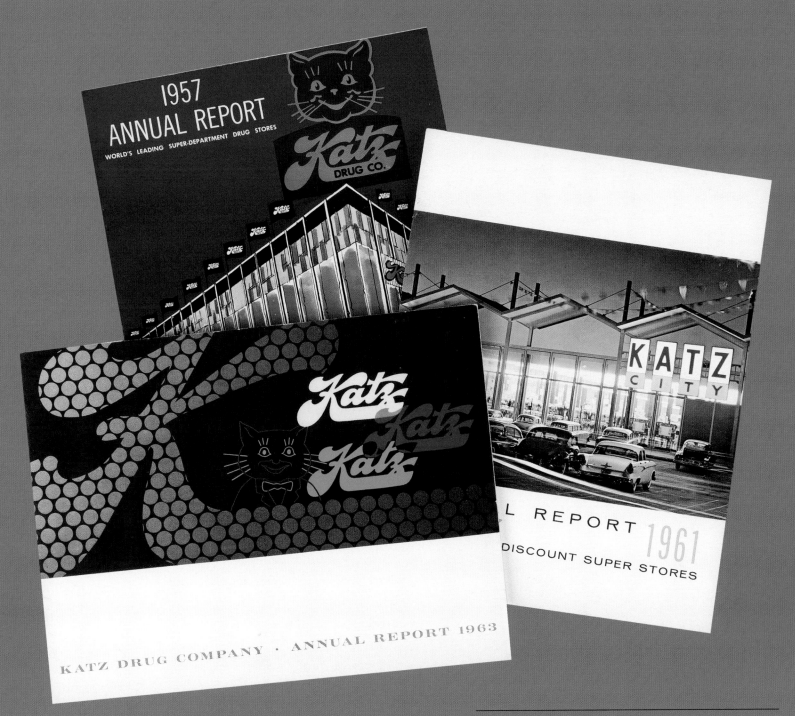

The company's annual reports almost always bore good news, including many photos of new stores in the chain.

Later that month, Katz turned that particular offer down. The next month Katz Drug, then operating 40 stores in five states, made another bet with a three-year expansion program.

The new stores would be, again, big.

"Through giant-sized stores with a wide assortment of merchandise, a pattern for profit has emerged," Shlensky said.

RENTING SPACE?

But that summer the company made an entirely new kind of announcement, this time deciding to join forces with the larger discount stores. It announced it had negotiated to operate leased departments inside three Fan Fair department stores in the Denver area.

Katz Drug would operate tobacco, cosmetics, candy, camera supplies and greeting cards departments inside the stores. They would be in states where Katz had never been before such as Texas (Dallas and San Antonio), Illinois (Collinsville), Connecticut (Hartford), Arizona (Scottsdale and Phoenix, where Isaac and Minnie Katz had begun making their winter home in the 1950s) and even as far away as California (Covina).

Maybe that was what had brought Michael Katz out to California the previous year.

The company borrowed $1 million to finance these depart-

> ## "WE HAVE QUITE A REPUTATION AS PUSHERS."
> ### — HARDWARE SUPERVISOR FRANK HOFFMAN

ments and kept fine-tuning.

For example, that single two drawer cash register in the Houston tobacco department. What were they thinking?

"This is wrong," read the 1961 memo Al Diamond wrote.

"One register should definitely be for service, the other register should be for self-service. Two drawers on one register will definitely slow up traffic in Houston."

And another thing: the third week of every month in Houston is a poor week, with lower volume, and the store manager should schedule his employee hours accordingly.

And be alert to the width of store aisles "in which women have enough space so that two merchandise carts can pass each other without crowding…"

And be consistent with discounts from department to department. "The trouble with most unsuccessful discount places today is that each department tries to chisel and raise their prices, hoping that the other departments will draw in the traffic."

"This is a good way to get killed."

It was difficult, Diamond added, in both Houston and Covina. In the latter store, he wrote, the "line-up of merchandise was deplorable and must have been very embarrassing and our competition probably could not understand our physical set-ups and alignment of merchandise when they came to see our operation."

As for the manager of the Houston store, Diamond added, "he is very poor in observation. He is very poor in seeing what must be done in the store and the writer believes this is due to his being fatigued and overworked, and feels that with things down to normal we will definitely see an improvement."

There were headwinds.

In August 1962, Katz omitted a quarterly dividend for the first time since 1938, which the company blamed on "uncontrollable circumstances."

That was one phrase for it. The real problem was the state's Sunday sales law, the same law which had been selectively enforced in St. Louis when Katz entered the

Many businesses, especially banks, glommed on to the idea of giving away free calendars. Katz designs were infectiously cheerful.

As business contracted during the '60s, there were some board meetings punctuated by disagreement on what the way forward should be, and gavel-pounding.

retail market there in 1936.

The law, first enacted in 1826, had gone largely unenforced in Kansas City and St. Louis, where Katz's competitors had pressured public officials into action.

NEVER ON SUNDAYS

In 1961, the U.S. Supreme Court upheld a Sunday sales law. Then, in January 1962, the Missouri Supreme Court upheld the old state law, effectively eliminating Sunday sales in the 27 Katz Drug stores in Missouri.

Yet the actual enforcement of the law varied from county to county across the state, resulting in what Morris Shlensky called a "chaotic situation."

It grew only more so. The Missouri Supreme court soon reversed itself, declaring the state's 19th century Sunday sales law un-constitutional. Then the Missouri legislature passed a new law.

In May 1964 the Missouri Supreme Court unanimously dismissed a claim by Katz Drug that the new law was vague.

Sunday sales issues apparently contributed to a malaise among

Katz electrical department managers, who convened in March 1963 to discuss a decrease in business. While the "Sunday selling problem" was on their agenda, the managers vented about other issues.

> "THE COMPANY
> WAS DOING
> $50 MILLION IN SALES
> AND MAKING
> PRACTICALLY NOTHING."
> — BOARD MEMBER
> BILL GLIKBARG

There was a general feeling, they said, that Katz stores "had no hot items."

A reduction in employees had been noticed by both employees and customers, as the managers believed the Katz reputation was becoming "can't get waited on" and "fewer sales people than ever before to handle the same amount of floor space."

An apparent reduction in inventory had been noticed as well, contributing to a perception that the long-standing belief that customers "can find everything at

Katz executives
Morris Shlensky
(right) and Earl Katz
led the company
in the 1960s.

In 1961, just months before Michael's death, the University of Missouri-Kansas City announced plans for a new Katz pharmacy building on campus.

Katz is no longer true."

While the company would rise to meet the Sunday sales challenge, there was another issue.

In December 1963, Morris Shlensky — not only president of Katz Drug but also the head of the National Association of Chain Drugstores — was indicted, accused of perjury in lying about alleged payoffs to Teamster officials. Three Teamster figures had testified that they had received payoffs every month from Shlensky from 1955 through 1961 in exchange for labor peace between the Teamsters and Katz.

But a jury found Shlensky not guilty the following April. Shlensky thanked the jurors and, after they had left the courtroom, wept.

The company made another bet that April — to mark its 50th anniversary with a $5 million expansion plan. It was the largest expansion in company history.

In 1967 the company announced it would build a Katz Discount City in Hutchinson, Kansas. At the end of the year, Katz Drug would be operating 44 stores in four states, 13 additional stores that it had acquired when it purchased a small chain called Crank Drug, and nine leased operations.

One strategy the company had adopted proved wise. Throughout the 1950s and '60s Katz chose to build away from downtowns, to follow changing population patterns as the federal interstate highway program made the exodus to the suburbs all the easier.

A REDUCTION IN EMPLOYEES HAD BEEN NOTICED BY BOTH EMPLOYEES AND CUSTOMERS.

The population of Johnson County, Kansas, just to the west of the Kansas City, Missouri, city limits, had grown from 63,000 to 123,000 during the 1950s.

But even with so many of its stores well positioned in the suburbs, growth seemed ever more elusive for Katz Drug executives, who would grow divided as to the best path forward.

Bill Glikbarg, husband of Michael

Katz's daughter Charlene and in the early 1960s a member of the Katz Drug board, remembered a key moment during an early 1960s board meeting.

"The company was doing $50 million in sales and making practically nothing," said Glikbarg. He remembers recommending that Katz re-mark, or slightly increase the prices, of many items on their stores' shelves.

According to Glikbarg, Morris Shlensky disagreed, saying that Katz Drug had been built on the reputation of being the lowest price in town and that he felt it would be a serious mistake to mark up prices.

The board deadlocked at three to three before Arthur Mag, longtime Katz legal counsel and then chairman of the company board, supported the motion to mark up prices.

"He [Mag] picked up the gavel, said 'Motion carried,' slammed down the gavel and walked out of the room," Glikbarg said.

The prices were duly marked up, and profit margins ticked up accordingly.

By the early 1970s Katz Drug operated about 65 stores, including the leased departments, with a sales volume of more than $100 million a year.

BRING IN THE CAVALRY

The company had endured and grown in an increasingly competitive environment. But the task perhaps had grown too difficult for the current staff.

"My feeling was that it would take outside management to do the job that needed to be done," Glikbarg said.

Steve Katz, grandson of Isaac, also felt the company was running in place. Delegated to overseeing leased departments within the Woolco chain, Steve Katz had grown frustrated about their prospects.

"They just didn't work for us," he said.

"They didn't allow us to make our margins and everybody was cutting everybody else in the throat. Everybody felt like they had to have a rock-bottom price. You couldn't run a pharmacy in those days and make money for the company." Wal-Mart, meanwhile, had opened its first store in Rogers, Arkansas, in 1962.

Steve Katz believed that Katz Drugs had built its reputation on

The cover of the free 1969 calendar harkened back to Katz Drugs' first focus: filling prescriptions, selling remedies and consulting on customers' health problems.

Above all, Isaac Katz understood human nature, including the motivating power of a handful of unspent nickels.

price and customer service. Katz customers, meanwhile, appreciated the service but ultimately were more interested in price. It would have required, he added, a prohibitive investment to re-tool that Katz Drug chain into a self-service retailer.

Steve Katz also agreed that there was a leadership issue. His father Earl was growing ill by the late 1960s, he said, and the vision of Isaac and Michael Katz, both now deceased, was growing more difficult to discern.

In December 1970, shareholders of Katz Drug and the Skaggs Drug Centers of Salt Lake City approved a merger.

At the time, Skaggs operated 88 retail stores in 13 states in the western U.S. Katz Drug operated 64 retail locations. The merger agreement mandated the exchange of 1.25 shares of Skaggs common stock for each share of Katz Drug.

On the basis of the more than 1 million shares of outstanding Katz Drug stock, Katz shareholders were scheduled to receive shares worth about $31.5 million.

It had been 57 years since Isaac and Michael Katz relocated from

Kansas City's West Bottoms. More than that since the brothers had perfected their low-price/high volume strategy across from the old Union Depot, using the nickel as its basic unit of currency.

WHAT IT TOOK

Michael Diamond, grandson of Al Diamond, one afternoon in 2011 told a story that had been told him many times by his grandfather. The story, Diamond felt, made vivid the savvy retail skills of the two Katz brothers, as well as their understanding of their customers.

"Their fruit stand in the West Bottoms was a long narrow establishment with beautiful fruit on both sides of the aisle," Diamond said.

"Everything cost a nickel. The cash register was in the back and all the change was given in nickels. That meant that if you bought a piece of fruit with a dollar you were handed 19 nickels.

"And then, as you would walk out the length of the store, you would be walking past everything that was priced at a nickel — and you would be holding a handful of nickels.

"It was genius."

WE'VE GOT MAIL

MEMORIES

DEAR KATZ,

Before this book was published, we asked Kansas City Star readers to send us their memories of Katz Drug stores.

If these emails are any indication, you made a lot of friends in your day.

Through two wars and a depression, people say you stocked pretty much everything they needed — and maybe a few things they didn't — with low prices and good service.

Just reading between the lines, it seems like you provided jobs and life training, gave people a place to hang out and get acquainted, and even find the love of their life.

Here are just a few of the more than 500 emails we received.

We hope you enjoy them.

THE EDITORS

To: KC Star
Cc:
Subject: Katz Drug Store Memories

Around 1940, when I was about 6, I was wondering what I could get for my folks for Christmas with the $2-$3 I had saved from my summer of picking berries. Katz's Christmas ads advertised all sorts of specials from glassware to cigars. There must have been close to a dozen items that I was able to buy, from "depression glass" salt & peppers, dishes for pickles, fruits, butter, etc., some perfume, and yes, a small box of cigars. My folks were amazed at all the things that I had been able to get for them that Christmas -- all from Katz coupon items!

Wil Larkin
Williamsburg, Va.

To: KC Star
Cc:
Subject: Katz Drug Store Memories

In the late '50s and early '60s, the Katz store at the corner of Swift and Armour roads in North Kansas City was the highlight of the town.

I remember going there with my mom to get a wide variety of things from toilet paper to complicated items such as pot holders. Going downstairs was more of an adventure than a shopping trip. The things they had down there were just amazing. Things you wondered "what the heck are these for?" and things you were sure could only be found at Katz.

One vivid memory is of my math teacher at North Kansas City High School, Mr. Moore, telling me if I didn't start paying attention and doing better I was going to end up working at the liquor department at Katz. That was all I needed to get my act together, for a few days.

Richard Winkler
Kansas City, Mo.

To: KC Star
Cc:
Subject: Katz Drug Store Memories

Getting off the 39th Street bus with my dad and older sisters on Monday afternoons was always one of the highlights of my week in the early '70s. I was 6 years old and, growing up in midtown, these trips to Katz made me for awhile at least forget that we were a poor black family.

While my mom went to her second job, daddy would treat us on his day off. I would go upstairs and get a hot wheels car or some baseball cards. (Wish I had those now.) My oldest sister would get makeup or a record (those round plastic discs, for those too young to remember) and my middle sister the artist always got some kind of art supplies.

We would end the outing by going to the counter, sitting down and having a soda while my dad socialized with the employees. Katz provided memories that I will never forget.

John White
Columbia, Mo.

To: KC Star
Cc:
Subject: Katz Drug Store Memories

The Katz Drug Store in Independence, Missouri, was located at Main and Maple. As you walked into the store there was a large swordfish hanging above the stairwell. My Uncle Elwood Huntsucker caught that fish, and it was too big for his house after it was mounted. A friend of his told him to take it to the manager of the Katz Drug Store and they would probably display it. When he told them about his catch they said, sure, they would love to have it. It was on display for about 25 years.

Betty Ballew-Swendrowski
Independence, Mo.

178

Until I turned five, my family lived in a house on Independence Avenue. There was a Katz store on the corners of Independence and Hardesty avenues, where I loved to shop with my Mom. One time I picked out a toy that was about $5 (a lot in those days) but Mom informed me she didn't have the money.

We continued shopping, me downcast and pouting, when low and behold I spotted a $5 bill on the floor.

My Mom was fairly certain that someone watching the scene dropped the money for me. Needless to say, I walked out of the store with my toy. I don't remember the toy but I sure do remember finding that money.

Diana (Crain) Caraher
Kansas City, Mo.

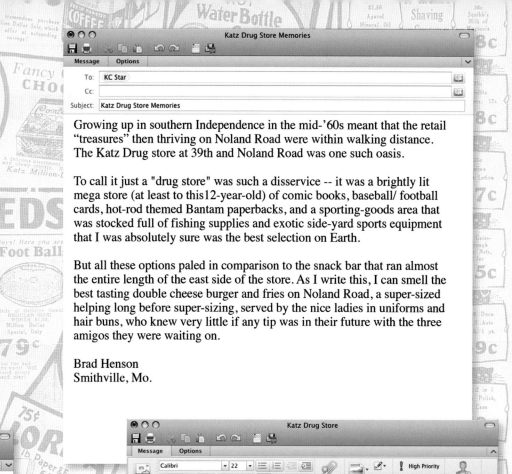

Growing up in southern Independence in the mid-'60s meant that the retail "treasures" then thriving on Noland Road were within walking distance. The Katz Drug store at 39th and Noland Road was one such oasis.

To call it just a "drug store" was such a disservice -- it was a brightly lit mega store (at least to this 12-year-old) of comic books, baseball/ football cards, hot-rod themed Bantam paperbacks, and a sporting-goods area that was stocked full of fishing supplies and exotic side-yard sports equipment that I was absolutely sure was the best selection on Earth.

But all these options paled in comparison to the snack bar that ran almost the entire length of the east side of the store. As I write this, I can smell the best tasting double cheese burger and fries on Noland Road, a super-sized helping long before super-sizing, served by the nice ladies in uniforms and hair buns, who knew very little if any tip was in their future with the three amigos they were waiting on.

Brad Henson
Smithville, Mo.

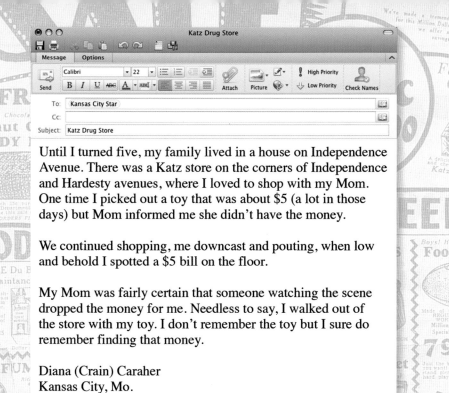

was a young man of 21, looking for a job. The year was 1959 and I had just gotten married. There was an ad in the Star. I went and interviewed, and was awarded the job, at a starting salary of $195 per month; gasoline was at 25 cents a gallon. They sent me to my job at store #41 at 75th and Metcalf in Overland Park, Kansas, where the store manager was Ray Jones.

started in the hardware department. Every store had its own Department Manager, Assistant Manager, Merchandiser and Buyer. The Manager and Assistant Manager would wear a suit and tie. The male employees wore white shirts and ties with red Katz jackets and the women wore dresses with red Katz jackets.

After I had worked there for two or three days, the manager Ray Jones came down the stairs to the hardware department where I was working. I was standing there and not doing anything. I had done all of my dusting and straightening of merchandise and filling the bins with new merchandise.

He asked me if I didn't have anything to do and I said "no" because I had done all of my work. Mr. Jones said that I needed to keep busy and proceeded to take all of the merchandise off of the island and put it on the floor, and said, "Dust it and put t back on the shelves. Do you understand? Keep busy."

Ray Hinton
Grandview, Mo.

I grew up in Independence and remember well the Katz Drug Store on the corner of the Independence Square, where my family often shopped. One Christmas the store had a display with a huge bag of M&Ms candy. I loved M&Ms! My sister and I did not have the money for this big bag. But on Christmas day, it was under the tree with my name on it. My sister had saved her money and bought it for me.

Thelma Sword
Independence, Mo.

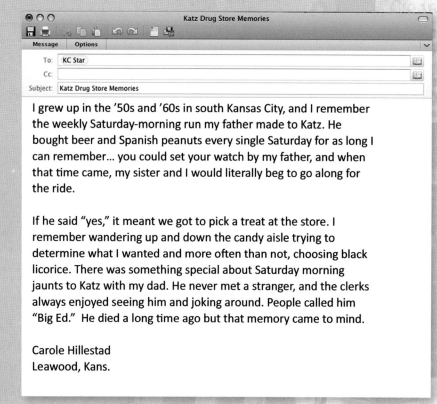

Subject: Katz Drug Store Memories

I grew up in the '50s and '60s in south Kansas City, and I remember the weekly Saturday-morning run my father made to Katz. He bought beer and Spanish peanuts every single Saturday for as long I can remember… you could set your watch by my father, and when that time came, my sister and I would literally beg to go along for the ride.

If he said "yes," it meant we got to pick a treat at the store. I remember wandering up and down the candy aisle trying to determine what I wanted and more often than not, choosing black licorice. There was something special about Saturday morning jaunts to Katz with my dad. He never met a stranger, and the clerks always enjoyed seeing him and joking around. People called him "Big Ed." He died a long time ago but that memory came to mind.

Carole Hillestad
Leawood, Kans.

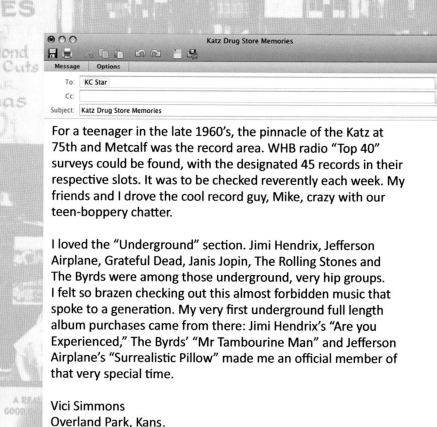

Subject: Katz Drug Store Memories

For a teenager in the late 1960's, the pinnacle of the Katz at 75th and Metcalf was the record area. WHB radio "Top 40" surveys could be found, with the designated 45 records in their respective slots. It was to be checked reverently each week. My friends and I drove the cool record guy, Mike, crazy with our teen-boppery chatter.

I loved the "Underground" section. Jimi Hendrix, Jefferson Airplane, Grateful Dead, Janis Jopin, The Rolling Stones and The Byrds were among those underground, very hip groups. I felt so brazen checking out this almost forbidden music that spoke to a generation. My very first underground full length album purchases came from there: Jimi Hendrix's "Are you Experienced," The Byrds' "Mr Tambourine Man" and Jefferson Airplane's "Surrealistic Pillow" made me an official member of that very special time.

Vici Simmons
Overland Park, Kans.

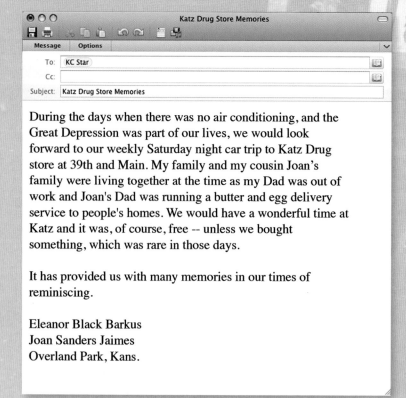

Subject: Katz Drug Store Memories

During the days when there was no air conditioning, and the Great Depression was part of our lives, we would look forward to our weekly Saturday night car trip to Katz Drug store at 39th and Main. My family and my cousin Joan's family were living together at the time as my Dad was out of work and Joan's Dad was running a butter and egg delivery service to people's homes. We would have a wonderful time at Katz and it was, of course, free -- unless we bought something, which was rare in those days.

It has provided us with many memories in our times of reminiscing.

Eleanor Black Barkus
Joan Sanders Jaimes
Overland Park, Kans.

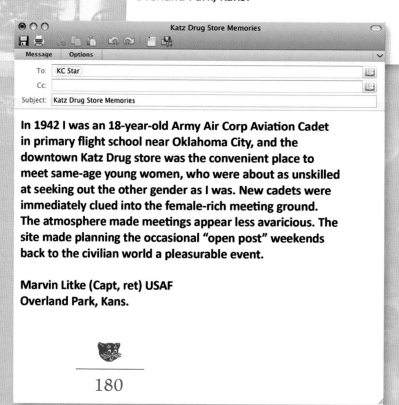

Subject: Katz Drug Store Memories

In 1942 I was an 18-year-old Army Air Corp Aviation Cadet in primary flight school near Oklahoma City, and the downtown Katz Drug store was the convenient place to meet same-age young women, who were about as unskilled at seeking out the other gender as I was. New cadets were immediately clued into the female-rich meeting ground. The atmosphere made meetings appear less avaricious. The site made planning the occasional "open post" weekends back to the civilian world a pleasurable event.

Marvin Litke (Capt, ret) USAF
Overland Park, Kans.

Message | Options

To: KC Star
Cc:
Subject: Katz Drug Store Memories

The Brookside Katz was a place where kids from Border Star and Southwest would go to meet. During the early '60s there was a locally famous dog named Rags that guarded the front door. He was shaggy looking and smelled a little rank. But he was friendly and always got a pat on the head and maybe some food from people leaving the drug store. This went on for a few years but one day he just disappeared and no one knew what happened. After that, going to Katz was never the same.

John Wilson
Osage Beach, Mo.

Message | Options

To: KC Star
Cc:
Subject: Katz Drug Store Memories

When I was about 13, my friend Jerry and I would walk to the Katz at 75th and Wornall, go in, and set the wind-up alarm clocks as a joke. We would set one for about 5 minutes later so we could hear it, and laugh. Then, we would set one for about 5 minutes after closing time so it would start ringing while they were trying to check out and close. We would set one more for the next morning before they opened, for the same reason.

We thought that was funny! Seeing the reactions of the people when it went off was hilarious! I also bought my first Beatles record at Katz in Raytown, and many model kits. They were great stores.

Wayne Goebel

Kansas City, Mo.

Message | Options

To: KC Star
Cc:
Subject: Katz Drug Store Memories

worked at the 40th and Main Katz store during my senior year in high school in he early '50s. My first assignment was in the Pet Department on the lower level. One day I was cleaning out the various pet cages. As I opened the door to the monkey cage, the monkey made a leap for freedom and was loose. He (or she) started up the main flight of stairs to the first floor and kept right on going up to the op floor and out an open window. A crowd was watching and I thought I was in ig trouble.

opened a door leading to the roof and, sure enough, the monkey had climbed a lag pole and was perched on the top looking at me. I studied the situation and nade a decision. I returned to the lower level and retrieved a step ladder and a long ish net from the Sports Department.

returned to the roof area, carefully placed the ladder under the monkey and started lowly climbing the steps. The monkey was eyeing me warily and, I could tell, was onsidering another leap.

Before that happened I reached out with the fish net and nabbed him (her). Wow -- retreated down the ladder and down the steps to the pet department with the nonkey in tow while the gathered crowd started clapping and cheering. I received little chewing out from my manager for being careless -- but I could tell she was ind of amused by the whole thing. As I live and breathe this is a true story.

Iarold Hatch
Kansas City, Mo.

Message | Options

Calibri | 22

Send | B I U ABC A AB | High Priority | Low Priority | Attach | Picture | Check Names

To: Kansas City Star
Cc:
Subject: Katz Drug Store

I remember in 3rd and 4th grade, going to the Katz on 50 highway in Raytown. My folks wouldn't buy us comics (12 cents at the time) so we would sit there next to the comic rack on the floor and read them for hours. The nice lady who worked in that department said she didn't mind at all as long as we were respectful and treated them carefully.

Vickie Brown
Blue Springs, Mo.

To: KC Star
Cc:
Subject: Katz Drug Store Memories

I worked at Katz Drug Store in the soda fountain department for several years beginning in the spring of 1952. I was 15 years old, and rode the school bus to Katz and worked from 5 p.m. until close, which was 10:45 p.m.

My favorite memory is meeting my boyfriend (now my husband of 56 years) at Katz. He worked at a garage/filling station on the block and would come over for the lunch specialty – the Royal Hamburger (1/4 pound), French fries and Coke for 39 cents. He also loved their chocolate malts -- I believe they were 20 cents. We also served full meals, usually meatloaf, mashed potatoes and vegetables, or similar items.

All of the employees had a fun time working there. Everyone knew everyone and enjoyed just taking some time with their friends.

Chuck and Arliss Elliot
Roeland Park, Kan.

To: KC Star
Cc:
Subject: Katz Drug Store Memories

My father, Virgil Geschwind, worked for the Katz Drug company in the late '30s and the early '40s. As a young boy, in the late '50s I remember him telling stories about working there and Mike and Ike Katz.

One of his favorites involved the hiring of a new security guard by the warehouse supervisor. The supervisor instructed the guard to allow NO ONE to enter the facility without a special ID card. One day one of the Katz brothers came to the warehouse and attempted to pass the guard, without an ID card. When the guard refused entry, the Katz brother yelled his name and insisted he be allowed entry. The guard said, "I do not care who you are, you are not getting in here without the card."

Mr. Katz was furious as he left and hunted down the supervisor. When he reached the supervisor and told him the story, he finished with the command, "Give that man a raise!"

Patrick Geschwind
Lee's Summit, Mo.

To: KC Star
Cc:
Subject: Katz Drug Store Memories

During my childhood in northeast Kansas City, I always looked forward to our weekly trips to Katz Drug store on Independence Avenue. The main purpose of these trips was for my Father to purchase his weekly supply of Roi-Tan cigars and my Mother to purchase the needed toiletries for the household.

But quite often a special trip to Katz needed to be made for a technical matter. My Father was not very handy around the house nor very technical, but when the TV went out he became a Rocket Scientist in my eyes. He would pull the back off the TV, remove all the tubes, place them in a brown paper sack, and ask me if I would like to go with him to Katz to check out the tubes. OF COURSE was my answer.

Sitting in Katz was this 8-foot-tall futuristic looking machine. My dad would scan the charts and books adjacent to the device to locate the correct socket out of numerous selections on the machine's surface. Once the correct socket was located he placed the tube in the socket to be checked. Then he would turn several knobs and slide levers to their "prober" setting. With dials and levers in their prober position he would hit the test button. The needle gauge and varying colored lights would reveal the status of the tube.

This process was repeated with each tube in hopes of finding that one bad tube. More often than not, one or two tubes would show a weak or bad status. At the bottom of the futuristic apparatus was a cabinet with replacement tubes assorted by their size and number. My Father would locate the correct tubes needed, purchase them and back home we would go.

Larry Johnson
Gladstone, Mo.

To: KC Star
Cc:
Subject: Katz Drug Store Memories

During my junior and senior years at North Kansas City High School, 1956-58, I worked part-time during the school year and full-time in the summer at the North Kansas City store. Mainly, I remember the friendly yet businesslike atmosphere in the workplace.

Everybody from the clerks to the managerial staff knew exactly what they were doing and exactly what needed to be done. The people-handling and cash-handling techniques I learned there served me well throughout my working life. Even though the wages were usually just a hair above the minimum, I never regretted one hour of the time I spent as a Katz employee.

Alan Hurlbut
Wichita, Kan.

In the late 1940's, I worked as a "soda jerk" at the Katz Drug store in Waldo.

One evening at closing time the manager told me to put the cat out. I was somewhat puzzled as I had never seen a cat in the store. I began looking for a cat and calling "kitty, kitty." The manager came to me and said, "I thought I told you to put the cat out."

I replied, "Yes, you did, but I can't find it." He calmly walked over to a wall switch, flipped it to the "off" position and the big Katz logo on top of the store went out.

Naturally, I felt like a dunce.

Rudy E. Ruechel, Jr.
Kearney, Mo.

My grandparents met while my grandmother worked at Katz at 40th and Main. Here is the story my mother wrote about that time:

"In the late 1930's, we attended St. Paul's Episcopal Church at 40th and Main. We shopped at Milgram's grocery store and Katz Drug Store, across from each other. In the '40s and '50s, my widowed father, Ernest Church, was the leader of the youth group at St. Paul's. After the meetings a group of us would go across the street to Katz to the soda fountain and visit.

While we were there one evening one of the employees, Muriel Wymer (a widow), came and sat down and began visiting. We soon learned that her son, Don, had just left to serve in the Army and wouldn't be home for Thanksgiving. My father proceeded to invite her to come to our house for dinner and she came. She and my father began dating and on Sept. 14, 1956, they were married.

Nancy L. Matteson
South Kansas City, Mo.

After graduating from high school in 1956, I went to work at the Katz Drug at 40th and Main. I was assigned to work the candy counter and that first week we were to do an inventory of all the candy. There were no computerized cash registers that kept track during those days, so everything had to be counted by hand. When we were finished, I was called into the manager's office and informed about the Cherry Mash situation.

It was believed that someone was stealing these yummy chocolate and cherry confections. The previous inventory showed that two boxes were missing, and the inventory I was part of showed that two additional boxes were unaccounted for.

Along with my other duties, I was on Cherry Mash watch.

One day, while bent over cleaning the glass cases, I saw a German Shepherd dog come through the front door, run straight for the candy counter, snap up one Cherry Mash, and run back out the door.

We moved the dog's favorite treat to the top shelf and ended his obsession and our problem.

Valerie Gilmore Gadberry
Hutchinson, Kan.

In 1967, I'd graduated from UMKC with a degree in Applied Art. I wanted to be a cartoon film animator, but the Vietnam War was raging and my student deferment had expired. I was classified 1A and no one would give me an art job, knowing I would soon be drafted.

I ended up applying at the brand new Katz Store at the new Metcalf South Shopping Center to work in their film department. They were the only place that would hire me and with my interest in film and art, it was a good temporary fit. And, since I'd owned motorcycles from the age of 14, I spent my lunch hours "scrambling" in the empty fields across Metcalf on the west side, where the Venture Store was yet to be built.

My draft notice came shortly and I quit December 15th to spend the holidays with my family, and shipped out January 15, 1968. I really felt a debt of gratitude to Katz Drug Stores, for giving me several months of work when nobody else would!

Bob Bliss
Prairie Village, Kan.

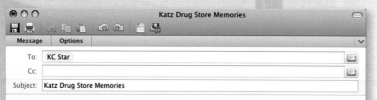

I was a pitcher and member of the Katz Druggists Baseball team, which was a member of the Ban Johnson League. We were sponsored by Katz Drug stores, which contributed much to the development of young people in the Kansas City area.

In 1953 we were Ban Johnson League champions. We then defeated Benson Manufacturing for the city championship in two games. I have a baseball used in game two, and I still have my red warm-up jacket with the blue cat icon on the front. Lew Denny was the team manager and Pat Nolan was the team coach. Both men were role models for the players.

Jim Foster
Olathe, Kan.

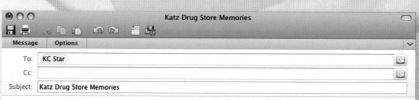

It was 1948 when Bob and I met at Westport High School. A friend of ours introduced us outside of Mr. Shearer's physiography classroom. We started dating, would meet after school, walk up 39th Street and south on Main Street to Katz drug store. Our favorite place to go for a coke and snack.

Katz drug store was built on property where the Harris Kearney house once stood on the Santa Fe Trail. In the 1800's wagon trains traveled through Westport. The house was later moved to 4000 Baltimore and is now the Harris Kearney Museum. Bob's family built the house.

If we hadn't gone to Katz, where our relationship grew, we couldn't tell that we married in 1951, have two sons, Bob and David, and a granddaughter Whitney. We just celebrated our 60th anniversary. What a fun place. THANKS KATZ!!

Bob and Joy Kearney
Olathe, Kan.

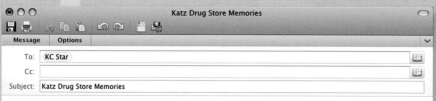

The first real job I had before my junior year of high school was as a fountain boy at Katz Drug at 10th and Main.

My definition of a real job: You filled out an application at the Katz Drug offices on the second floor above the 12th and Walnut Street store, were interviewed, and got hired.

That summer I trained and worked, making malts, shakes, sodas, and hundreds of limeades, a specialty drink during the hot summers. You kept 10 to 15 limeades half made up ahead of time in fountain glasses with metal holders, one squeezed lime and one squirt of simple syrup. Upon order, you added ice and carbonated water.

You also made the simple syrup. You brought a large stock pot filled with water to a boil, added 10 lbs. sugar and stirred until dissolved. When school started I did the same thing at the 39th and Main store, working Saturdays and Sundays.

I believe the pay was 75 cents per hour.

Albert Amborn
Olathe, Kan.

I remember this time in my life very well. I no sooner became employed in the Accounts Receivable department at the company offices at 12th & Walnut, when I became very ill with strep throat and couldn't work for almost two weeks. After I returned, a very nice man in Accounts Payable asked me for a date. His name was James J. (Jim) Bateman and on September 12, 1948, we were married.

Since couples weren't allowed to work in the same office, I left to seek other employment. Jim continued to work there for many years. I particularly remember the quarterly inventories, counting by hand every single item in the stores and warehouse. Times have sure changed.

Mary Ruth Bateman
Kansas City, Mo.

My mother and her future mother-in-law worked at Katz in St. Joseph. My father was on leave from the Navy and visited his mother to have lunch at the store. He ran into my mother and they were married a year later. They had gone to grade school together in Martinsville, Missouri. Then my father's family relocated to St. Joseph where he graduated high school. They didn't meet again until 6 years later! I remember trips to the drug store as a small child to visit my grandmother. They are all gone now, but I will never forget that is where my parents met in a brief moment and spent almost 40 years together until my mother passed in 2000.

Helen Hurley
Independence, Mo.

While I was growing up in Independence during the 1950s and '60s, my dad was a sales representative for the Larus Brothers Tobacco Company, and the Katz Drug Store chain was one of his biggest clients. I can remember every Saturday getting up and loading the company car with the latest order from the store. We would then go upstairs and get dressed up to head up to the square. (You could never go without being dressed properly.)

We would walk in with our products, and my dad would meticulously start going over his display in the front of the store. After this long procedure, we would walk to the back to the soda fountain. The waitresses all dressed in their uniforms would gleefully shout, "Here's Al with his daughter." They would come and take our usual order—one cup of black coffee and one tall ice cream soda. They would converse about the goings-on of the world while I sipped so slowly every drop of the most delicious soda you could ever imagine.

Next we would head downstairs to the yard and garden supply area, and we would never leave without going to the toy section where I was allowed to pick out something to take home.

You see for me, the Katz Store was not just another store—it was a special place for my dad and me.

Later, when my father passed away, I remember going to pay my last respects before the funeral. When I turned around, in the doorway was a lady dressed in a fur coat. She introduced herself and said she was one of the waitresses at Katz and how much they would all miss my dad—and, I bet they really did—just like I miss going to the Katz store every Saturday with him.

Betty Kurtz
Independence, Mo.

In 1928 (I was about 5), my super-enterprising Dad was building "crystal set radios" in the basement of our home at 3863 East 59th St. One day, I fell down the steps (hit my head), to come face-to-face with a bushel basket of crystals he had assembled in ½-inch lead holders he had poured. Remember the copper tuner coil with headset earphones? That was "the radio" for about two broadcast choices.

Sometime later, from a demonstration he made for both Katz brothers, Dad got an order for 144 sets -- which scared him to death. Could he actually build 144 sets for about $2 each? I am sure my mother thought he couldn't. My recollection, 83 years later, is that he was "saved" by the new vacuum tube radio that wiped out the crude crystal set radio business. He always admired Ike and Mike Katz.

Frank R Schultheis, Jr.
Pleasanton, Kan.

On Saturdays in the 1950s, our parents would drop my brother Don and me at the Katz store in North Kansas City, where we would eat lunch, then go downstairs to the pet department to look at all the puppies, kittens, fish, etc.

Then Don and I would go to the Armour Theater and get in for a quarter apiece since we were under 12, and we would see two movies, cartoons, previews and newsreels, entertaining us for nearly six hours. Pretty cheap babysitting for our parents.

But that was a more innocent time.

Bob and Don Hughes
Versailles, Mo.

To: KC Star
Cc:
Subject: Katz Drug Store Memories

I started working for Katz Drug Co. at age 18, as a Comptometor Operator in the fall of 1947. I was in the Accounting Department at the Armour Road location, and later moved to the main office at 12th & Walnut. I lived in Kansas City Kansas, and walked to the street car stop at 18th & Minnesota, then transferred to the bus at 10th & Grand. I always wore a dress or skirt and heels, and was never late except for one time when, as I was walking to the streetcar stop, a bird pooped on my head and I had to return home to wash my hair. Before I could even get back on my way to work, someone from the office had called to check on me -- I was the youngest in the office and they all mothered me. My bosses, Mr. Erickson and Mr. Bateman came to my wedding. I stayed with the Katz company until April of 1953 when I left to start my family. I still have my 5-year Katz pin with the emerald eyes. It was a great place to work and I loved every minute of it.

P.S. I have yet to find anyone who knows what a comptometor is -- a kind of prehistoric calculator! I attended a special school to get my certificate for it.

Betty Sutlick Elson
Olathe, Kan.

To: KC Star
Cc:
Subject: Katz Drug Store Memories

I had the good fortune to grow up in the greatest era in the history of our great nation, commonly referred to as the '50s. And the good fortune to be able to ride a bicycle from Independence, where I was born and raised, to Kansas City and all points in between.

One of our favorite stops was Katz on the square in Independence. Unlike today, there were no bike racks, and bikes were pretty much strewn all over the sidewalk. I doubt store management today would allow the number of kids running around in their store that Katz did in the late '40s and '50s. I'm not sure how often we were in Katz, but it was many times a week.

Charlie Shriver
Fountain Hills, Ariz.

To: KC Star
Cc:
Subject: Katz Drug Store Memories

Some of my favorite memories involve the Katz Drug Store at 75th St. and Metcalf. I am the oldest of six, all born in nine years. My Dad and I used to drive over and check on the building while the store was being built. I was about six or seven, and I loved this alone time with Dad. It looked so big, so modern and had so much glass that we could watch in the evening and see the workers. When it finally opened we could not wait to have a look. Sometimes we would go up and get a cherry phosphate or some other yummy thing.

My Dad died when my youngest sibling was just two, which left my Mom with six young children. She kept up the Katz tradition though. If she had to go pick something up she would sometimes pick just one of us to go with her. That was very precious time alone with her.

When we got older, we could walk up to Katz with a friend or sibling. That is when you knew you were really big. As you can see, many of my best childhood memories had to do with Katz Drug Store.

Linda Dunn
Shawnee, Kan.

To: KC Star
Cc:
Subject: Katz Drug Store Memories

In 1969, when I was in college in Springfield, Missouri, I was making a typical Saturday night run to the liquor department at Katz. Loaded down with bottles of inexpensive wine, I came around the corner of an aisle and was confronted by a large gorilla! I screamed and dropped the bottles, breaking several. It turned out that the gorilla was just a guy in a realistic costume. I had forgotten that it was Halloween. The manager was very nice. He had seen the whole thing happen and knew my shocked reaction was genuine. I have a chuckle about my close encounter with that gorilla every Halloween. And considering how hard he was laughing at the time, I bet the guy in that gorilla costume remembers the encounter as well!

Linda Daily
Kansas City, Mo.

In 1958 my Mother, I, my younger sister, younger brother, and baby brother walked from Cypress to the store at 31st and Van Brunt. We bought my first comic book (Superman/Bizarro) at that store, and we bought cold cuts for supper at the Justrite grocery store right next door.

My first job was making signs in the Katz store at 31st and Van Brunt. I set type, made signs, cleaned type, posted signs. Hated that job. Fumes were horrendous, and the ink got onto everything. Later on, I was promoted to assistant manager of the Sundries department.

Mother was co-manager of the cosmetics department (same store) for a number of years. I was in the store one night and chased a shoplifter down Raytown road towards Leeds. I had on leather-soled wingtips. He stopped, and I tried to. Slipped and evidently was knocked out because the next thing I was aware of was walking back to the store.

Richard W. Brown Jr.
Grandview, Mo.

In the late '60s when I was 10 to 12 years old, my Mom would get her Social Security check every month (she was legally blind) and we'd ride the city bus to this area which she referred to as "the avenue" and do a little shopping.

We'd go to the Katz store at Main & Westport Road, and I remember we'd sometimes eat at the little restaurant that was inside the store right next to the music area. They served great tasting cheese burgers and fries. That's where my Mother bought me my very first record album newly released: "Abbey Road, The Beatles." Since then, I have a love of their music and others.

Thank you Mom, love you, miss you.

Patrick Gordon
Oak Grove, Mo.

When I started painting watercolor renditions of buildings, cityscapes and architectural elements, the first paintings I wanted to do of the Kansas City area was the Katz Building on Main.

Ms. Lee Knox
Kansas City, Mo.

I began my working career at 18 years old in the Katz Drug flagship store at 75th and Metcalf. I started in the garden center which was located on the lower level. The year was 1969. Most of the employees were older, many in their 50's, 60's and 70's. Many of them had worked for Katz for 30-40 years.

I did about every job that was available downstairs such as garden center clerk, sporting goods, pets, hardware, etc. I moved up quickly within the organization because of the great lessons I learned from the older, wiser managers.

We had many great customers in those days, one of whom was the family of Jan Stenerud, kicker for the Chiefs. Many of the Katz family also shopped there. A big part of the surrounding neighborhood used to eat at the in-store restaurant and order the day's Blue Plate Special as they listened to live 45's and albums being played by Ron Condie in the adjacent record department. Many times adults and teenagers played the pin ball machine located next to the restaurant.

During holidays I was the designated singer. I would sing the Katz theme song over the intercom: Shop and Save, It's So Easy When You Shop At K-A-T-Z, That's KATZ!

Jeff Richman
Arlington, Texas

MORE THAN A STORE

By Norma Virden

THROUGH THE LATER YEARS of the Great Depression, two wars, and new beginnings, the Katz Drug stores were much more than the place where my family bought medicine.

Often times, when there was not 40 cents for the four of us to go to the picture show, Dad would drive mom, my sister Wilma and me in the old Chevy three blocks to Katz in Waldo. He would go in and purchase a big 12-cent bag of popcorn for us to share as we "watched the people" and discussed their merits.

On special occasions we were treated to a trip to the big 39th and Main Katz Store. It had everything a person could need and very much that a person just wanted. It was a Depression child's Disney World.

My first part-time job was at Katz in Waldo, sacking oranges. Twelve oranges for less than a quarter. The lines were so long we didn't have time to look up or notice that Mr. Mike or Mr. Ike was our next "customer," checking to see that all was running smoothly. My job made it possible to help my family by paying for my school books and if there was a little left, maybe a pair of the popular white moccasins which sold for $2.98. At 15 cents an hour, it took awhile.

The soda fountain was our after-school social gathering place. One coke, two straws. Never a disturbance. The boys were gone to war.

Bill and Norma Virden celebrated their 50th anniversary at St. Matthew's Lutheran Church in Lee's Summit. It was 51 years after their wartime engagement, Christmas Eve 1948.

The Virdens with their son, Mark, whose arrival provided the impetus for this story's end.

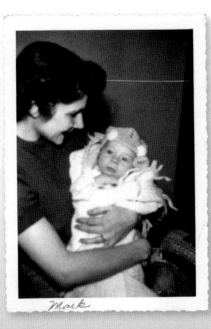

Mark

Above left, Bill in front of their new Plymouth. Norma, right, holds Mark the December day they came home from the hospital. Below, Norma, left, and a friend in front of their G.I. house.

Of all the wonderful memories involving Katz the most cherished was Christmas 1950. The love of my life came home and on Christmas Eve 1948 gave me an engagement ring. Then on Nov. 12, 1949, we were married.

In spite of all the precautions available at the time, the Lord decided to bless us with a bouncing baby boy on Nov. 24, 1950. With the news of his impending arrival, we purchased a brand new G.I. house. So with house payments, car payments, doctor bills and only one salary now, not a penny was to be had for Christmas presents for anyone.

Christmas Eve was extremely depressing. About eight o'clock, my wonderful Bill said "Get your coat and bundle up baby. We are going for a ride." He drove to Katz in Waldo. He took out his wallet and fished around and pulled out a $2 bill. He said "I have been saving this since the Philippines. You go in and buy me a present for $1 and then I will go in and buy you one for $1."

Christmas suddenly became beautiful. I bought him a pocket knife that he carried until his death six years ago, and he bought me a green wool headscarf which is in my cedar chest clearly marked "My Christmas present from Bill bought at Katz Drug Store on December 24, 1950."

Norma Virden wrote a long-running column, Smoke Signals, for Kansas City's Country Squire magazine. She and Bill started the Model T Club of Kansas City and together restored Model T cars, which they drove to meets across the country. She lives in Lee's Summit, Missouri.

ACKNOWLEDGEMENTS

Brian Burnes wishes to thank: Chris Wilborn of Wilborn & Associates who tracked down archival photos of Katz Drug stores and then produced beautiful prints on a tight schedule; Chuck Haddix and staff at the Marr Sound Archives at the University of Missouri-Kansas City, who provided us with recordings of Katz radio commercials from the early 1960s; staff members at the Herbert Hoover Presidential Library & Museum in West Branch, Iowa, who provided the photograph of a young Herbert Hoover; the staff at the Harry S. Truman Library and Museum at Independence, Missouri, whose holdings include the oral histories of Truman colleague and Kansas City drug store executive Tom Evans, and Derek Donovan and Eric Winkler at the Kansas City Star Library, who retrieved for us many archival Kansas City photographs.

Thanks, also, to Colleen Roberts, who told of her father's career at the Katz Drug Company, which included planning the 1954 grand opening of the company's new store in Memphis, Tennessee, and hiring, Colleen said, the young Elvis Presley for an opening night concert; Margie Morrison, who told us about her husband's time with Katz, which also included a stint at the Memphis store; Michael Diamond, who recalled several stories told him by his grandfather and Katz executive Al Diamond; Bill and Charlene Glikbarg, who shared memories of Charlene's father, Michael Katz, as well as Katz board meetings long distant, and Steve Katz, grandson of Isaac Katz, for the whole opportunity to begin with.

Carol Powers wishes to thank: The Star readers whose memories of Katz Drug stores were, without exception, worth publishing; Norma Virden and her son, Mark, for the story of Christmas Eve 1950; Dan Stolper for the gift of an unpublished memoir written by his wife's great uncle, Lewis Jay Navran, whose keen recounting of the Michael Katz kidnapping was a priceless resource; Opal Walker for going to see Elvis Presley perform in a Memphis parking lot in 1954, and taking snapshots of the King.

Thanks, also, to Kansas City Star graphics artist Dave Eames for his professional acumen and cartographic skills; Jeremy Drouin for his help in securing so many pertinent images from the Kansas City Public Library's Missouri Valley Special Collections; Janet Weaver at the Iowa Women's Archives at the University of Iowa Libraries for the image of Edna Griffin; Beverly Mosman and Terry Zinn at the Oklahoma Historical Society Research Division for pictures of the Oklahoma City sit-in and Clara Luper; Tiffany Patterson at the State Historic Preservation Office in Jefferson City for the time-consuming retrieval of images of the Michael Katz house.

And Steve Katz, for the opportunity to learn about his family's journey, and whose spirit is in every page of this book.

DJ Matheny wishes to thank: Aaron Leimkuehler, advertising photographer at The Star, for his talent and inspired collaboration that resulted in so many evocative images; Jo Ann Groves, for her consistently upbeat and supportive help with photographic and production issues; Lee Kester, whose father worked in sales promotion at Katz Drug, for her generous provision of original annual reports and other memorabilia; Steve and Ward Katz, as well as Steve's daughters, Laura Katz Stang and Jennifer Katz Krause, for their gracious cooperation in allowing us multiple visits to their homes, in search of all sorts of Katz memorabilia — and for the lending of same, and Jon Henderson, whose love and appreciation of period graphics inspired the design of this book.

And most of all, thanks to Ed Matheny, my husband, without whose generous and patient support of my efforts, the design of this book would not have been possible.

Brian Burnes, a St. Louis, Missouri, native, has been a staff writer for The Kansas City Star since 1978. He is the author or co-author of several Kansas City Star Books titles, including *High & Rising: The 1951 Kansas City Flood, Walt Disney's Missouri: The Roots of a Creative Genius*, and *Harry S. Truman: His Life and Times*. He and his wife Debra live in Westwood, Kansas, with their children Charlie, Jessica and Sam.

For Steve Katz, writing the story of his Grandfather, Isaac Katz, has been a journey of almost 30 years. His persistent research reveals the history, beginning in Imperial Russia, of an amazing American family. Steve graduated from Dartmouth College, and is himself a former Katz Drugs executive. He has written several books on cycling. He lives in Leawood, Kansas, near his own six grandchildren.

Sheffield Cemetery, 6200 Wilson Road, Kansas City, Missouri
Final resting place of Frank and Sarah Katz,
parents of Isaac and Michael

*They came in ships to a young, unproven country.
They left everything, risked everything, and in so doing
added depth and fire to the dream known as America.*

th & Grand, Kansas City, Missouri | 12th and McGee, Kansas City, Missouri | 728 Minnesota, Kansas City, Kansas | 601 Francis, St. Joseph, Missouri |

nsas City, Missouri | 4th & Pierce, Sioux City, Iowa | Main & Robinson, Oklahoma City, Oklahoma | 7th & Locust, St. Louis, Missouri | Hodiamont & Easto

ost, Kansas City, Missouri | 63rd & Brookside, Kansas City, Missouri | 6150 Natural Bridge, Pine Lawn, Missouri | 75th & Broadway, Kansas City, Missouri

souri | Armour & Swift, North Kansas City, Missouri | Gregory & Prospect, Kansas City, Missouri | 201 N. Main, Independence, Missouri | 52nd & Roe, M

va | 2256 Lamar, Memphis, Tennessee | 441 N. Kirkwood, Kirkwood, Missouri | 9005 E. 50 Highway, Raytown, Missouri | 8959 Riverview Blvd., St. Louis, M

1st & Van Brunt, Kansas City, Missouri | 7501 Metcalf, Overland Park, Kansas | 115 W. 29th, Topeka, Kansas | 8571 Watson Road, Webster Groves, Miss

ugs, Sedalia, Missouri | Katz Drugs, Hutchinson, Kansas | East Hills Regional Shopping Center, St. Joseph, Missouri | Elms Shopping Center, Joplin, Misso

a, Kansas City, Kansas | 601 Francis, St. Joseph, Missouri | 10th & Main, Kansas City, Missouri | 7th & Locust, Des Moines, Iowa | 12th & Baltimore, Ka

lahoma | 7th & Locust, St. Louis, Missouri | Hodiamont & Easton, Wellston, Missouri | 15th & Cleveland, Kansas City, Missouri | 3030 Prospect, Kansas

dge, Pine Lawn, Missouri | 75th & Broadway, Kansas City, Missouri | 6th and Edmond, St. Joseph, Missouri | 8th & Washington, St. Louis, Missouri | Manc

y, Missouri | 201 N. Main, Independence, Missouri | 52nd & Roe, Mission, Kansas | 954 Minnesota, Kansas City, Kansas | 50th & May, Oklahoma City, C

05 E. 50 Highway, Raytown, Missouri | 8959 Riverview Blvd., St. Louis, Missouri | 3124 Raytown Road, Kansas City, Missouri | 100 E. Euclid, Des Moines,

15 W. 29th, Topeka, Kansas | 8571 Watson Road, Webster Groves, Missouri | 6312 Prospect, Kansas City, Missouri | 460 N. Lindberg, Florissant, Missour

pping Center, St. Joseph, Missouri | Elms Shopping Center, Joplin, Missouri | Watson & Elm, St. Louis, Missouri | 7401 Manchester, St. Louis, Missouri |

nsas City, Missouri | 7th & Locust, Des Moines, Iowa | 12th & Baltimore, Kansas City, Missouri | 12th and Walnut, Kansas City, Missouri | 40th & Main, Ko

ssouri | 15th & Cleveland, Kansas City, Missouri | 3030 Prospect, Kansas City, Missouri | Independence & Hardesty, Kansas City, Missouri | Linwood & T

mond, St. Joseph, Missouri | 8th & Washington, St. Louis, Missouri | Manchester & Sutton, Maplewood, Missouri | Independence & Prospect, Kansas C

nsas | 954 Minnesota, Kansas City, Kansas | 50th & May, Oklahoma City, Oklahoma | 4701 Sycamore, Roeland Park, Kansas | 1900 Carpenter, Des M

124 Raytown Road, Kansas City, Missouri | 100 E. Euclid, Des Moines, Iowa | 1925 S. Third, Memphis, Tennessee | 12236 S. 71 Highway, Grandview, M

2 Prospect, Kansas City, Missouri | 460 N. Lindberg, Florissant, Missouri | 1735 S. Glenstone, Springfield, Missouri | 1635 Poplar, Memphis, Tennessee |

tson & Elm, St. Louis, Missouri | 7401 Manchester, St. Louis, Missouri | 8th & Grand, Kansas City, Missouri | 12th and McGee, Kansas City, Missouri | 72

y, Missouri | 12th and Walnut, Kansas City, Missouri | 40th & Main, Kansas City, Missouri | 4th & Pierce, Sioux City, Iowa | Main & Robinson, Oklahoma

ssouri | Independence & Hardesty, Kansas City, Missouri | Linwood & Troost, Kansas City, Missouri | 63rd & Brookside, Kansas City, Missouri | 6150 Natu

ton, Maplewood, Missouri | Independence & Prospect, Kansas City, Missouri | Armour & Swift, North Kansas City, Missouri | Gregory & Prospect, Kans

701 Sycamore, Roeland Park, Kansas | 1900 Carpenter, Des Moines, Iowa | 2256 Lamar, Memphis, Tennessee | 441 N. Kirkwood, Kirkwood, Missouri | 9

rd, Memphis, Tennessee | 12236 S. 71 Highway, Grandview, Missouri | 31st & Van Brunt, Kansas City, Missouri | 7501 Metcalf, Overland Park, Kansas |

ne, Springfield, Missouri | 1635 Poplar, Memphis, Tennessee | Katz Drugs, Sedalia, Missouri | Katz Drugs, Hutchinson, Kansas | East Hills Regional Shoppin

y, Missouri | 12th and McGee, Kansas City, Missouri | 728 Minnesota, Kansas City, Kansas | 601 Francis, St. Joseph, Missouri | 10th & Main, Kansas City

Pierce, Sioux City, Iowa | Main & Robinson, Oklahoma City, Oklahoma | 7th & Locust, St. Louis, Missouri | Hodiamont & Easton, Wellston, Missouri | 15t

3rd & Brookside, Kansas City, Missouri | 6150 Natural Bridge, Pine Lawn, Missouri | 75th & Broadway, Kansas City, Missouri | 6th and Edmond, St. Jose

rth Kansas City, Missouri | Gregory & Prospect, Kansas City, Missouri | 201 N. Main, Independence, Missouri | 52nd & Roe, Mission, Kansas | 954 Min

emphis, Tennessee | 441 N. Kirkwood, Kirkwood, Missouri | 9005 E. 50 Highway, Raytown, Missouri | 8959 Riverview Blvd., St. Louis, Missouri | 3124 Rayto

nsas City, Missouri | 7501 Metcalf, Overland Park, Kansas | 115 W. 29th, Topeka, Kansas | 8571 Watson Road, Webster Groves, Missouri | 6312 Prospe

ssouri | Katz Drugs, Hutchinson, Kansas | East Hills Regional Shopping Center, St. Joseph, Missouri | Elms Shopping Center, Joplin, Missouri | Watson & E

nsas | 601 Francis, St. Joseph, Missouri | 10th & Main, Kansas City, Missouri | 7th & Locust, Des Moines, Iowa | 12th & Baltimore, Kansas City, Missouri

cust, St. Louis, Missouri | Hodiamont & Easton, Wellston, Missouri | 15th & Cleveland, Kansas City, Missouri | 3030 Prospect, Kansas City, Missouri | Ind

ssouri | 75th & Broadway, Kansas City, Missouri | 6th and Edmond, St. Joseph, Missouri | 8th & Washington, St. Louis, Missouri | Manchester & Sutton, Mo

Main, Independence, Missouri | 52nd & Roe, Mission, Kansas | 954 Minnesota, Kansas City, Kansas | 50th & May, Oklahoma City, Oklahoma | 4701 Sy